GLOBALIZATION AND ARTISANS

GLOBALIZATION AND ARTISANS

BY

DR. CH. SRUTHI

KALPAZ

First Published, 2019

Published by

Kalpaz Publications
C-30, Satyawati Nagar,
Delhi – 110052
Ph.: 011-47034999, 9811692060
www.kalpazpublications.com
E-mail: kalpaz@hotmail.com

Printed at: G. Print Process, Delhi

Cataloging in Publication Data—DK
Courtesy: D.K. Agencies (P) Ltd. <docinfo@dkagencies.com>

Sruthi, Ch., author.
Globalization and artisans / by Dr. Ch. Sruthi.
pages cm
Includes bibliographical references and index.
ISBN 9789353240189

1. Artisans—India—Telangana. 2. Caste—India—Telangana. 3. Arts—Economic aspects—India—Telangana. 4. Arts and globalization—India—Telangana. I. Title.

LCC HD8039.A542I4 2019 | DDC 338.63 23

Contents

Preface ... 7
Foreword ... 9
Acknowledgment ... 11
List of Tables and Figures ... 13
Introduction ... 15

1. **Artisan History** ... **17**
2. **Theoretical Perspectives on Caste** ... **61**
3. **Globalization- An Introduction** ... **89**
4. **Methodology** ... **109**
5. **Globalization and Artisans: Impact Analysis** ... **119**
6. **Findings and Conclusions** ... **155**

Bibliography ... 173
Index ... 185

Preface

This book is a contemporary attempt to review the scholarly literature on the status, position, cultural economics, green economics and ethnic production of Artisans in general and Artisans in Telangana region in particular. In this Globalized era, a meaningful analysis of the Artisan sector requires focusing on particular geographies and crafts. For a comprehensive understanding of the current status of the Artisan sector in Telangana region of Southern India, it is important to understand the Artisan value chain. The artisanal value chain depends on *Human Resources, Legal Entities, Credit Facilities, Technology, Transport to markets, Quality checks, Marketing and Promotion of goods.*

The two important concepts – Structure and Function – imply that every society is whole and that its various parts are interrelated. The *Structural – Functional* perspective relies more on the field work tradition for understanding the social reality of the artisanal caste occupations, so the present study can be understood as 'contextual' or 'field view' perspective of the social phenomena in Telangana region. The study intended to fulfill the evident gap of knowledge regarding, how artisanal production contains within itself the incredibly rich heritage of the region, its culture and its role in maintaining social and economic stability of society. The study encompasses artisans: as major resource of skills for innovation and creativity, capable of lifting Global competitiveness.

The study intended to develop a unique and contextual understanding of globalization and observes its implication on the considered artisan caste occupations of Telangana. Further, social dynamics of artisanal caste occupations of Pottery, Weaver and Blacksmith, which consists of major role of women, in the advent of globalization are given due importance. The book has been presented in six chapters, namely *Artisan History, Theoretical Perspectives on Caste, Globalization-An Introduction, Methodology, Globalization and Artisans: Impact Analysis, and Findings and Conclusions.*

Dr. CH. SRUTHI

Foreword

The law of nature is the law of change. Human societies had remained dynamic, prone to changes in its constituent sub systems, caused by endogenous or exogenous forces. Change had always had been ubiquitous. The changes precipitated by Globalization in the last decade of Twentieth century had been of varied trajectory and intensity. It has virtually swept across continents like a Tsunami on the globe affecting each and every society and its constituent segments. The forces unleashed by the processes of Liberalization, Privatization and Globalization (LPG) caused extensive sway on the Institutions, Cultural, value spheres displacing the traditional agriculture, weaving, and the handicrafts throwing them off-gear from their traditional moorings. It is almost two decades since the LPG tide has swept the globe in various vicissitudes.

It is in this context that the present work authored by Dr. Ch. Sruthi tries to document the plight of the artisans like the Weavers, Potters and Blacksmiths in the state of Telangana, who remained entrenched in the traditional arts, which were once the pride of the culture of the region.

The researcher has traversed the Telangana region to document and vividly portray the prevalent scenario covering the current status of the arts, artisans and their lives and the changes visible in their social firmament. It is one of the finest research studies undertaken at the right time to capture the extent and intensity of change sequel to the process of Globalization.

I hope that this book would kindle the readers to come out with ameliorative initiatives to save the dying arts and the artisans from extinction and preserve them for the posterity.

Let me congratulate Dr. Ch. Sruthi on publishing this research work, which I am sure would benefit the Administrators as a feedback, NGOs to plan initiative to uplift the artisans and the researchers more such studies to evolve suitable initiatives to revive and save these priceless arts and artisans and stem the process of their extinction. I deem it as a privilege to write this foreword for the wonderful book. Wishing the book a wider reach and reading.

Professor Amarnath R. Das
Department of Sociology
Sri Krishnadevaraya University

Annathapuramu
Andhra Pradesh

Acknowledgement

The author expresses her heartfelt thanks and deeply indebted to her parents and her in-laws for their encouragement throughout her life. The author is grateful for the support and guidance of following academicians: Prof. Ch. Sanjeeva, Prof. K. Muralimanohar, Prof. G. Ramulu, Prof. C. Ganesh, Prof. T. Ramesh, Prof. T. Srinivas, Dr. A. Ailiah, Dr. M. Swarnalatha. They made many wise and valuable suggestions.

The author is indebted to : Prof. K. Siva Kumar and his wife Dr. Neelaveni madam, Dr. N. Narsimlu and his wife Dr. Kavitha, Dr. D. Sreenivasu, Dr. B. Raju and his wife Dr. Saritha for their untiring support and relentless encouragement. The author is extremely thankful to publishers. Finally,from bottom of the heart, the author expresses her thankfulness to Prof. Amarnath.R.Das, without his kind support, scholarly advice and encouragement , this work would not have been realised.

The author extremely indebted to her husband Dr. CH. Srinivas, and her daughters Lakshmi Sree, Shaarvani and Swetharca Chinmai for their spirit of accommodation, patience, co-operation and support, without whose support and co-operation this book could not have been materialized.

List of Tables and Figures

Tables

Table – 1(i) Details of funds allocated and funds utilized during last three years 37

Table – 1(ii) Scheme-Wise Funds Released Under Handicrafts Schemes in Erstwhile Andhra Pradesh State 38

Table – 3(i) Education in India - Globalization 105

Table – 4(i) Zones of Telangana State 113

Table – 5(i) Age wise classification of respondents of Pottery 125

Table – 5(ii) Educational Status of Respondents of Pottery 125

Table – 5(iii) Income-wise Distribution of Potter Respondents 126

Table – 5(iv) Potter Respondents Engaged part-timely on other works 127

Table – 5(v) Nature of the Houses of Respondents of Pottery 127

Table – 5(vi) Adoption of Technology by Respondents of Pottery 128

Table – 5(vii) Age wise classification of Weaver respondents 133

Table – 5(viii) Educational Status of Weaver Respondents 133

Table – 5(ix) Income-wise Distribution of Weaver Respondents 134

Table – 5(x) Weaver Respondents Engaged part-timely on other works 135

Table – 5(xi) Nature of the Houses of Weaver Respondents 136

Table – 5(xii) Adoption of Technology by Weaver Respondents 136

Table – 5(xiii) Age wise classification of Blacksmith Respondents 142

Table – 5(xiv) Educational Status of Blacksmith Respondents 143

Table – 5(xv) Income-wise Distribution of Blacksmith Respondents 143

Table – 5(xvi) Blacksmiths Engaged part-timely on other works 144

Table – 5(xvii) Nature of the Houses of Blacksmith Respondents 145

Table – 5(xviii) Adoption of Technology by Blacksmith Respondents 145

Figures

Figure – 1(i) The Mammayee goddess 55

Figure – 4(i) Telangana State 112

Introduction

In the Stratified Indian Society every artisan caste occupation has a role in catering the needs of the society. Every caste has different tradition, a different need and a different competence. With the advent of industrialization and colonial rule, artisan fraternity has been adversely affected. Since then the consistent decline in the artisan production is quite evident from socio, economic waning of artisans.

The present era of Globalization pervades into the cultural traits of the society. The Globalization has brought with it more competition. Even though export is not the purpose of production, artisan productions need to be export worthy to survive. In the domestic market itself, many crafts have to compete with freely imported foreign goods.

Handicraft is the second largest source of employment in India after agriculture, and its growth performance especially in post liberalization has been impressive, still the sector remains misunderstood. Modernity i.e., adoption of ideas and ways of living that mimic the West have branded the indigenous traditional production as local and primitive. Thus there is a neglect and ignorance towards the value of the artisanal production, which has huge scale and potential towards rapidly changing markets and can hugely contribute to social and economic stability of the society.

The potential of handicraft sector and its growth prospects include its ability to act as a significant source of economy with knowledge skill, design aspect, along with basic nature to adapt to contemporary relevance. The challenges of global economy position the handicraft sector as a major resource of skill for innovation and creativity, capable of lifting India's global competitiveness.

The Artisan sector can be understood from both *macro* and *micro level* –i.e., taking its contribution to the Indian economy through export at *macro* level and in terms of its employment potential in *micro* level. In the *micro* level it could be accessed that Indian Handicrafts constitute a significant segment of the decentralized sector of its economy providing employment to millions of artisans of weaker sections hailing from OBCs, SCs, STs and Women.

Artisan Caste genealogy reveals the significance of its production in religious and cultural practice. Many production items have both use value and cultural value. Market / Globalization in any form, may come in conflict with the cultural standards. Neglect of the intrinsic and inherent value to owners/artisans resulted in discontent.

Tradition must be a *Spring-board* not a *cage*, and if product is to be utility based and economically viable, it cannot be static. Products are constantly evolving, but they must also respond to changes in markets, consumer life styles, fashions and usage (modern trends). In responding to these changes in markets, life styles and usages, it is the role of designers and other agencies that serve as mediators that assumes significance in sensitively interpreting these changes to the artisan people.

India has distinguished craft heritage, so the export of Indian handicrafts should not be seen as the only parameter of development of this sector. There should be a push from the domestic market. The biggest problem while implementing the developmental schemes is the lack of proper knowledge on handicraft units and number of artisans. Due to this the government apparatus is fractured and mired in historical aberrations. Now a complete census of the artisan is need for proper statistics, which enable the government to plan the appropriate mediations.

This work is an effort to analyze the livelihood and social aspects related to cultural significance, hidden scientific and eco-friendly nature of indigenous artisanal caste production of traditional artisans pertaining to *pottery, weaving* and *black smithy* along with exploring the changing artisanal caste professions in the advent of globalization in Telangana.

Chapter - 1

Artisan History

The notion that artisans and their crafts existed as timeless cultural artifacts in bounded communities was echoed in early ethnographic studies of Indian villages. The early anthropological pursuit in India, which was initially conducted under the aegis of classifying the natives, imagined as primarily constituting village republics, organized in the recital with the principles of *Brahmanical* Hindu world view. These anthropological studies had strengthened this ideal of India through village ethnology of the caste system with in bounded villages, without paying much attention to the impact of colonial policies and interventions on the construction of caste identities.

In subsequent historical and anthropological work, it has been shown that the *Jajmani system* was perhaps an invented tradition and not a original marker of the traditional village.

The prominent studies on Occupational Cluster have emerged largely in the Anthropological accounts of India. The traditional relationship between caste and occupation is a phenomenon observed and analyzed closely by social anthropologists like *Dube* (1955), *Bailey* (1957), *Lewis* (1958) and *M.N. Srinivas* (1959-1996) etc., some even trying to propound an occupational theory of the origin of caste [1, 2, 3, 4.]

'The Handicrafts and Industrial Arts of India' by *Rustam J. Mehata* (1960) reveals the handicrafts and their historical linkage to different places in India. The pottery, clay-figures, folk toys, wood carvings, stone carvings etc., have been given clear indications about their origin and nature, the superiority they carry for Indian culture and civilization[5].

'Handicrafts in India' by *T.M. Abraham* (1964), describes about different crafts of the country. The analysis of the rise and fall of the handicrafts in the Indian Society, the author has described its role in the country's economy and how instrumental handicrafts are in unifying the India's culture and glorifying its civilization, gave a historical understanding of Indian handicrafts in a cogent manner[6].

Emphasizing on the greater value of the arts and crafts, *T.M. Abraham* wrote: "the world of art and craft is as valuable as the world of science, philosophy or ethics. Like art, crafts reflect the state of human society through the individual. Craft treasures like arts give us a glimpse into the core and kernel of the collective mind and societies through the mirror of individual mind that created them".

'The Glory of Indian Handicrafts' by *Kamaladevi Chettopadhyaya* (1976), reveals an analysis of the major craft goods of all over India. This book give descriptions about crafts like, woven textiles, hand-painted fabrics, embroidery, carpet and floor-coverings, leather works, ivory, basketry, mats, bamboo and cane works, folk paintings, jewelry, pottery, etc. Though the books have no mentions about the concerned artisans and their social life, the authors take care of making the readers' understanding clear about different crafts of the country and the glory of Indian culture[7].

'Crafts and Craftsmen in Traditional India' by *M.K. Pal* (1978), gives important definitions and historical backgrounds of important crafts such as textiles, pottery, terracotta and jewelry, etc., with wide details. Apart from this, it emphatically narrates the socio-economic status of artisans in a proper historical manner, social and occupational stratification, an account of raw materials, traditional tools and production techniques have also been described in the book. The author has also given proper details of crafts and crafts persons and the institutions directly connected with the development of the crafts like the State Industries Department, handicrafts and handloom Export Corporations of India Ltd etc, along with necessary suggestions for the development of the traditional crafts[8].

There are numerous varieties of art crafts in India which are made with attractive designs and meticulous craftsmanship, highlighting the various Handicraft products produced by the artisans of the erstwhile Andhra Pradesh State[9].

Experts have characterized the key problem in the handicrafts sector as one of "vastly asymmetric information as well as asymmetric capabilities between the artisan and the market operators"[10].

India faces two major demographic realities which can make or break its development potential – the demographic dividend of a large youthful workforce facing a massive gap in skills and employability.

The case for the handcraft sector is supported by delayed recognition that economics is not a mathematical science but a creation of society and culture. This has been established by *Prof. Stephen Gudeman*, Chair, Professor of Anthropology, University of Minnesota in 'Economics as Culture: Models and Metaphors of Livelihood'. The idea that science and technology create objectivity and rationality, and that there is something different in the application of these principles that characterizes modernity, has been disproved by *Bruno Latour*, one of the world's most renowned sociologists from France, in 'We Have Never Been Modern'.

Developmental experts at the World Bank, International Monetary Fund (IMF), the UN agencies and Action Aid, as well as reputed sociologists and philosophers have turned a central focus to *culture* and specifically to crafts as a basis to rescue human society from the current economic morass and moral impasse[11].

There is therefore a need to look beyond the singular preoccupation with Gross Domestic Product (GDP) as the sole basis for understanding growth, and to reconsider why development planning in India is faced with such large and disturbing evidence of mal-development on several fronts in human and social terms. The case for the artisan must therefore be one of several efforts to ensure that the approach to the Twelfth Plan can go beyond mere statistics to encompass a broader understanding of human development within the opportunities unleashed by liberalization and the global marketplace, as well as a mature acceptance of its threats.

Prof. Michael Walton, Centre for Policy Research, Harvard University sees cultural industries as a 21st century industrial strategy and not as conservation activities – "No society achieves transition successfully without innovation and deep creative skills".

Chadha (1997) notes that while National Sample Survey (NSS) data show what percentage of the Rural workforce are employed in different gainful activities, there is no indicator of whether employment is in rural, semi-urban or urban areas[12].

Surveys do not capture the complexity of much rural employment share households and individuals may pursue a number of different activities, and employment patterns may vary both seasonally and across different years. *Fisher* identified 17 sub-sectors, which account for 80% of all Rural Non-farm (RNF) employment. The secondary sector includes many traditional sub sectors such as Textiles, wood, pottery, food, tobacco and metal products[13].

As part of major study of rural growth linkages, *Hezell* and *Haggblade* (1991) suggests the income from the Rural Non-farm studies contributes between 25% - 35% of total income of rural households, in contrast with its 20% - 25% share of employment[14].

Unni (1998) argues that the beginning of a structural change in employment away from Agriculture towards the non-form sector is evident, both at all-India and rural India levels[15].

Deshpande and *Deshpande* (1998), based on NSS data, well summarize recent patterns in the labour market, attributed to the impact of liberalization. They conclude that the demand for labour has increased with liberalization, but has not been shared evenly by rural and urban regions, by men and women, and by regular and casual workers[16]

Based on a study of secondary data from Census reports, National Sample Survey (NSS) and Planning Commission, *Shrivastava*et.al., (1995), examine the current status of the participation of female workers in rural non-farm employment and the trends, constraints and prospects they face[17].

Handicraft, like farming, is not premised on the guarantee of minimal returns. At the same time, individuals in these activities cannot exercise an option to withdraw their investments and fund the next '*Sunrise Sector*', for myriad reasons. They are forced to take recourse to belt-tightening. The wave of suicide among Indian farmers and weavers indicates a calamity hidden by national income calculations biased toward production and value addition in the so-called 'formal' sector.

Given these conditions, the crisis of data is not difficult to understand. It is a crisis in planning that has so far failed to bring together the range of economic, social, political, environmental, cultural and ethical concerns that are required for nurturing crafts as a "*sector of sectors*" of enormous future significance.

A common estimate of artisans in India is 6.5 million – a stock figure carried for long years in publications of the 'Development Commissioner (Handicrafts)' [DC (H)] and elsewhere. An estimate released in June 2011 was of 7.6 million, of which over 47% were women. National Sample Survey estimates made almost two decades ago suggested a figure of

8 million. The Eleventh Plan targeted 8 million in handicrafts and 7 million in handlooms, or a total of 15 million by 2012. This figure is close to an estimate made as long ago as 1982 by the late *D N Saraf*[18].

A source in the *Indian Institute of Foreign Trade* estimated 173 million of artisans in September 2009. Other estimates range between 100 and 200 million, perhaps one of these figures acknowledge that almost the entire adult population of regions such as the states of the North East and Kashmir comprises artisans, the finding revealed in this study that around 50% of all craft production may originate from women artisans. These huge variations have failed to attract serious attention.

Notwithstanding the absence of reliable data indicating a collective amnesia, the broad sweep of the sector's might is undeniable. The most casual reflection on the dimensions of the sector, publicized by conservative examination of available statistics, will reveal a staggering resource that demands attention. Employment is huge, in hundreds of millions. Craft Council of India (CCI's) considered guesstimate of the numbers of artisans at the core of the handcraft industry is 200 million.

An analysis of the national statistical databases, commissioned by CCI with the Madras School of Economics, returned a figure of 31 million artisans for 2001 Census, based on screening the National Industrial classification categories for handicrafts. This procedure and data-set only includes main workers. It excludes women working from home, as well as pre- and post- production processes, and possibly many artisans subsumed under various industrial codes for one reason or another. CCI applied an extrapolation factor corresponding to the findings of its pilot field study in Gujarat and Tamil Nadu, for adding back non – main workers, to arrive at a figure of 100 million. Given that one has no idea how many main workers are excluded by virtue of being subsumed under the wrong industrial codes, the figure of 200 million, derived from the Eleventh Five-Year Plan document, might be closer to the truth.

Employment figures for 2006-07 for handloom and handicraft are shown respectively as 124 lakh people in 2001 and 68 lakh people in 2006-07. This does not include handicraft artisans who may be currently counted under silk, unorganized wool, coir, Khadi Village Industries Commission (KVIC) and gems and jewelry (manufactured goods) categories in the Plan document. Two hundred million is the best 'reading' of current available statistics for the number of artisans in the handloom and handicraft sectors, although it refers to a non-standard definition and exclude large categories that are administratively categorized elsewhere. The real number may well be much larger.

Utilizing definitions developed by the Development Commissioner (Handicrafts), earlier crafts studies as well as UNESCO frame work's pilot study along with report of "CEIS: Preliminary Findings from Stage 2 – A Pilot Study of Two Clusters", has developed and applied the following definitions of handicrafts and artisans.

Handicrafts are products or services provided by artisans, working primarily with their hands. The artisan very often uses traditional knowledge and her/his direct manual contribution forms a substantial or distinctive part of the end product or service. Usually there are minimal or limited inputs from machines. The distinctive nature of handicraft comes from the fact that these goods or services can be identified with certain traditions or geographies.

An artisan is a person with special hand skills, often handed down traditionally across generations, and often linked to a complex traditional knowledge system encompassing the material, technology and/or design aspects.

1.1 Conceptualizing Artisans

The traditional handicrafts have evolved out of basic human necessity and not from an abrupt astral need. The evolution of handicrafts have utilitarian roots, the first object to receive human's artistic attention was a weapon. Handicrafts serve as an index of society's cultural refinement in its everyday activities, which reflects the sensitivity in the society's cultural response to material changes.

Irrespective of the religious affiliations, even today our Artisans who engage in making handicrafts observe a ceremonial vow or invariable a ritual associated with craft[19]. These traditions in Indian handicrafts which are still being adhered to by practitioners in their original form despite the ravages of time and history may be attributed to three principal sources namely, *the royal courts, religious arts* and *folk arts*[20]. In spite of adherence to age old traditions by the practitioners of traditional handicrafts, their inherent latent power of assimilation has helped the traditional Indian handicrafts to survive and flourish even today[21].

India has one of the most diverse and ancient traditions of handmade products and its handicrafts industry is an important economic and cultural asset. India's innumerable craft traditions and living craft skills are the vehicles of its cultural identity, passed on generation to generation and means of sustenance for numerous communities engaged in production. Artisanal production constitutes one of the primary subsectors within the creative and cultural industries, defined by UNESCO as "Industries which produce tangible or intangible artistic and creative outputs, and which have a potential for wealth creation and income generation through fostering of cultural assets and the production of knowledge : based goods and services"[22].

The expansive relationship between artisans and the nation-state is almost clearly demonstrated in the independence movements of 19th and early 20th centuries. In particular, it was Gandhi's *Swadeshi* movement which recognized the artisan as the catalyst of rural development. The symbolic power of *Khadi & Weaving* is synonym with the Nation's struggle against the Colonialism.

The rural artisan was someone who needed to be protected from modernity in the form of colonialism or later in the form of Globalization.

Though Gandhi's philosophy for Indian development was kept aside, in favour of Nehru's Industrial modernization programs, Gandhi's philosophy of promoting traditional village industries was still incorporated into national policy after independence. *Kamaladevi Chattopadhyaya* laid the path in establishing many of the leading government and non-government organizations for the development and advancement of the Handicraft sector, including the central cottage industries emporium and Craft Council of India.

India's Industrialization and participation in the modern world economy is decades old. But still millions of Indians depend on indigenous modes of production, traditional skills and techniques to make a living based on hand made products. These artisans are the backbone of non-form rural economy with an estimated 7 million artisans according official figures (up to 200 million Artisans) according to unofficial sources engaged in traditional caste occupation to earn a livelihood[23].

Majority of artisan production remains unorganized and informal with its full market potential untapped, especially by the artisans, who more often struggle for sustenance. Propelled by the loss of markets, declining skills and difficulty catering to new markets, a large number of artisans have moved to urban centers in search of low, unskilled employment in industries.

According to United Nations, since past 30 years, the number of Indian artisans has decreased by 30%, indicating the urgency to re-invest in artisans to safeguard history, culture and an important source of livelihood[24]. Harnessing the potential of the artisan sector to preserve traditional craft, strengthen the sector, and improve the incomes of artisans requires different types of investments that should focus and build corner stone of artisans' sustainability. They are,

(i) Establishing Artisan centered clusters through the value chain.

(ii) Increasing domestic demand for indigenous crafts and strengthening market linkages.

(iii) Strengthening the decentralized production model.

(iv) Statistical data base approach

During the British period Indian villages and their economy encountered a crisis. The Industrial Revolution which took place in 18th Century influenced our villages also. This revolutionized our traditional production system along with transport. The factories and Railways disturbed our indigenous village production. The factory production which was on huge scale and also cheaper made our village industries irrelevant. The village artisans became unemployed for their market was replaced by factory produce. The artisans in all cases were the losers[25].

The advent of *Industrial Revolution* brought a drastic Change in the economic structure that forced different castes to adopt occupations other than their traditional ones. Not able to with stand the machine made products which were not only very cheap, but also produced in bulk quantity with good quality, many of the rural families migrated to urban areas in search of jobs for their livelihood in factories. The other cause for the migration was sometimes epidemics. Much of migration was also resulted due to construction of dams (i.e., Dams & Displacement). Sometimes only men migrated to urban areas; women were left with unequal struggle for survival. Women who were passive movers to the urban areas along with their household head had to face all problems of unsettled life without even basic amenities which resulted in slum settlement, battering consequences due to changing attitudes of men, rise in domestic violence, high mortality rate, malnutrition etc.

In *Pre-Industrial* Indian societies occupations were caste based, families acted as economic unit. Most economic activity took place within the house hold, production and distribution were organized by customs and traditions.

The family as an economic unit has always been dependent on special labour done by family members. The family was a multi-generational producer with capital, land and tools provided by older generations and labour provided by younger generations. Family based productions of caste occupations which were not only limited to agricultural products but also produced manufacturing goods and provided services. Women as a daughter/mother/wife were actively participating in caste based occupations. As the production was home based women after completing their daily house-hold work used to make huge contribution in the production process[26].

1.2. Categorizing Caste Occupations

These occupational Caste groups can be categorized as

1. Artisan castes.
2. Service Castes.

The Backward classes community in Telangana consists of 92 Castes and these castes are categorized into four groups [27].

Group-A : 39 Castes.

Group-B : 21 Castes.

Group-C : Harijan Converts.

Group-D : 33 Castes

a. Artisan Castes

1. Viswa Brahmins / Vishwa Karmas
   - (i) Kammari (Black Smith)
   - (ii) Vadrangi (Carpenter)
   - (iii) Kanchanri (Brass/Bronze Smith)
   - (iv) Silpi (Sculptor)
   - (v) Kamsali/Ausali (Gold/silver Smith)
2. Salivahana/Kummari (potter)
3. Surya Balija
   - (i) Ganika (Dancer, Singer, poet)
   - (ii) Kalavantulu.
4. Weaving
   - (i) Anchukatlavandu

(ii) Dudekula
(iii) Devanga
(iv) Jandra
(v) Kurni
(vi) Neelakanthi
(vii) Kamabhakthulu
(viii) Koshti
(ix) Nakkala
(x) Patkar
(a) Khartri
(xi) Padmashali
(a) Neeli
(b) Sali
SalivanPadmasali
(c) Senapathulu
(xii) Karikalabakthulu
(a) ThogateSali
(xiii) ThogateVeera Kshatriya (Warriors)
(xiv) Veerakshitriya Swakulasali
(xv) Narasimha Caste.

b. Service Castes

1. Barber.
2. Washer.
3. Cobbler.

1.3 Defining Artisan

Utilizing the definitions developed by the Development Commissioner (Handicrafts), UNESCO frame works, has developed and applied the following definitions of Handicrafts and Artisans.

"Handicrafts are the products or services provided by Artisans, working primarily with their hands. The Artisans very often uses the traditional knowledge and his/her direct manual contribution forms a substantial or distinctive part of the end product or service. Usually there are minimal or limited inputs from machines".

"The distinctive nature of Handicraft comes from the fact that these goods or services can be identified with certain traditions or geographies."

"An Artisan is a person with special hand skills often handed down traditionally across generations and often linked to a complex traditional knowledge system encompassing the material, technology and/or design aspects."

An Artisan or craftsman is a skilled manual worker who makes items that may be functional/decorative, like furniture, clothing, jewelry, house hold items i.e., pots, vessels.

1.4 Understanding Indian Artifact Sector

Artisans were the dominant producers of consumer products prior to the Industrial Revolution. According to classical economics theory, the division of labour occurs with internal market development[28]. However, according to economist John Hicks, merchants and artisans originated as servants to the rulers.

During the middle Ages, the term 'Artisan' was applied to those who made things or provided services. Artisans were divided into two groups those who owned their own business and those who did not. Those who owned their businesses are called 'masters'. They enjoyed higher social status in their communities, and were most influential group among artisans and others were workers.

Real India resides in Rural India. A large portion of rural population in India depends on cottage industries for its Economy, which enables for having hugely preserved 'the cultural heritage of India' and helps the country to maintain its unique Identity. Artisanal caste occupations are small business carried on at home involving very less number of people as labourers who mostly are or sometimes may not be members of one family. Such a production/ manufacturing of goods involve those traditional artisans and craftsmen who have inherited their work as an art form from their previous generations.

Since ancient times in India such indigenous products have been able to attract foreign traders and merchants. They helped India in successfully establishing trade relations with the Greek, Chinese and Arab merchants. Even in medieval India, Indian craftsmen and artisans flourished well under the rule of Turks, Afghans and Mughal dynasties.

The Industrial Revolution gave a fatal blow to their Economy and led to a considerable decline in their number. Though, *'Swadeshi'* and the

'Boycott foreign goods' movements led by the then freedom fighters helped in promoting Khadi and other Indian fabrics to some extent, but could not help in saving the decline of manufacturing items that involved fine work as well as artistic taste.

Broadly, Artisans are divided into four categories with rigid hierarchical between more and less skilled artisans in particular craft.

(i) Skilled master artisans

(ii) Wage worker artisans

(iii) Fully self-employed artisans

(iv) Part-time artisans

The present craft sector demonstrating different stages in craft production, from production to market is as follows, however each craft will have a slightly different set of processes.

(i) Organization

(ii) Procuring and Processing Raw material

(iii) Production

(iv) Aggregation and Intermediary Trade

(v) Markets

(vi) Demand

i. Organization

Artisans are usually structured into groups through informal contracts between traders, master artisans and low-skilled artisans.

More formal system of artisan organization involves four main types of entities, *self-help groups, Mutually aided co-operatives, Producer companies (for profit legal entity) in companies bill in 2002, private limited companies*[29].

However, most artisans continue to work independently as there is a widespread lack of awareness about the advantages of being organized into the above forms.

ii. Procuring and processing raw materials

Traditionally raw materials used by artisans were locally available due to their close linkages in the village. The *Jajmani system*, which consisted of reciprocal relationship between artisanal castes and the wider village community for the supply of goods and services, provided artisans with access to community resources. The breakdown of traditional structures, along with competition from industry, it became difficult for the artisan to buy raw material at affordable prices, forcing them to rely on local traders who provide raw material against orders at high prices which forced artisans to switch to non-traditional raw material.

iii. Production

Though techniques and processes vary from craft to craft, production generally takes place in house-holds, with family members engaging in production process according to their capacities. Even in organized structures artisans typically produce within community settings.

Production is generally seasonal, with crafts activity being suspended during harvest season, as most artisans are also engaged in agriculture to supplement their livelihood.

iv. Aggregation and intermediary trade

Aggregation is bringing together products from decentralized production units to enable economies of scale in transportation, storage and retail. Due to improper (dismissal status) infrastructure and communication in India, aggregating products is a challenging task, leading to many bottlenecks in the craft supply chain resulting in loss of opportunities for artisans to access markets.

v. Markets

Markets for craft products are local, retail shops, fairs, *melas*, mainstream exhibitions and exports. Among these local markets are common for many artisans[30].

vi. Demand

With the advent of Globalization and availability of cheaper and more varied products, crafts face severe competition in contemporary market. They are typically perceived as traditional, old-fashioned and primitive to modern tastes.

There has been a limited efforts to reposition the image of crafts and build consumer appreciation of the history and cultural identity associated with hand made products.

Indian craft sector is in disarray, while crafts received royal and aristocratic patronage during pre-independence days, and played central role in independence struggle, they slowly lost relevance with the advent of Industrialization. In this globalized era the sector carries the stigma of inferiority, and backwardness, compounded by the government treating it as a sunset industry, i.e., illustrated in lack of well-developed policies and programs to protect and strengthen the ecosystem for artisan.

Problems of Indian Artifact Sector

The four main challenges artisans are facing in creating sustainable livelihood in today's economy are

i. Low Productivity

The informal nature of the sector and low education of most artisans create issues such as

(a) Un organized production – scarcity of professional infrastructure like sheds, storage space, shipping, packing facilities etc.

(b) Low education – As entire household participates in production to some capacity, and as it serves as seasonal source of income, their children miss schools, resulting in low education levels for the entire family making it difficult for them to

- Manage inventory
- Access government schemes
- get market information and bargain with trades and middlemen

The families which engaged in artisanal production, 50% family heads are having no education where as 90%women hailing from artisanal production are completely uneducated[31].

(c) Outdated production methods - Artisans lack financial capability to upgrade technology in production.

ii. In-adequate Inputs

There are three main reasons,

(a) *Lack of quality raw material* - Due to less quantity of Raw material requirement, they have low bargaining power and forced to buy substandard materials at higher prices.

(b) *Lack of Funding* - Artisans Lack working capital, access to credit and loan facilities. So, Unable to full fill the bulk orders and support their family needs. There are several government schemes intend to fill this gap for artisans through institutions like National

Bank for Agricultural and Rural Development (NABARD), Small Industries Development Bank of India (SIDBI). It is not only difficult for uneducated artisans to access these schemes but also inadequacy of size of loan, delay and extensive paper work necessary to acquire loan, forces the artisans to borrow from local money lender or trader or Microfinance companies at high interest rate. The All Indian Debt and Investment Survey -2002, showed money borrowed by rural households from money lenders rose from 17.5% in 1991 to 29.6% in 2002[32].

(c) *Lack of Design inputs* - In most traditional societies, design evolved with interaction between artisan and consumer and artisan was aware of socio-cultural context of the consumer. In the present globalized market, with increasing urbanization, artisans face difficulty in understanding the latest trends of the market and the changing demands; this in turn reflects the marketing of their produce.

iii. Information asymmetry

Due to less literacy, artisans cannot identify potential new markets for their product, nor do they know how to interact with these markets. This in turn reduces their understanding of market potential of their goods, the price of their product in different markets.

They are unable to avail various government schemes, welfare policies and diversification opportunities meant for their craft development.

iv. Fragmented value chain

(a) Lack of market linkages, consumers of craft products are increasingly becoming urbanized, crafts continued to be sold through local markets; artisans have few opportunities to reach new consumers.

(b) Dominance of middlemen

(c) Lack of Aggregation

Artisanal production takes place in scattered clusters in rural areas while markets are usually in urban centers. There is a lack of organized system to efficiently aggregate goods from small producers, carry out quality checks, storage facilities for approved goods and supply them to wholesalers and retailers in urban market areas. Thereby, it results in the loss of large percentage of market for artisans.

v. Lack of an enabling environment

(a) Neglect by central and state governments: Government views the sector as a sunset industry, so schemes designed for artisans tend to have low priority in terms of execution and assessment. Within crafts, the government's priorities are skewed towards the export market, with 70% of its crafts budget going towards development of environment to enable export[33.] Crafts sector falls under the purview of 17 different government ministers, ranging from the Ministry of Textiles to Ministry of Women and Children, results in confusion and in action.

(b) Lack of interest by second generation: Rural youth increasingly are not interested in continuing their caste occupation (family craft tradition) for three main reasons,

- Having seen their parents struggle to find markets and fair prices for their products, they are inclined to pursue other trades.
- Educational curriculum does not signify the importance of crafts and their cultural heritage;
- Rather it pushes towards white collar jobs.

Initiatives - Supporting Artisan Sector

K.K. Subramanian remarks India's unique craft heritage should not be merely a reminder of past glory but should be used as dynamic force to accelerate economic development. During post liberalization, the growth of tourism industry cultivated the notion of interior decoration and raised the demand for ethnic crafts, the traditional crafts were not powerful enough to influence the liberal imports of cheap machine made products and many other factors of globalization regime[34]

J. Stiglitz viewed that "the globalization today is not working, it is not working for many of the world's poor. It is not working for the much of the environment. It is not working for the stability of global economy. The problem however is not with globalization, but how it has been managed"[35]. So globalization is a reality that cannot be denied. To safe guard from its dim features, bringing common consensus in domestic/developing nations by curtailing the monopoly of the developed nations is needed.

Various efforts have been made by the Indian government, Private Sector and non-profits to address the challenges faced by Indian Artifact sector[36].

(i) Government Programmes

After Independence Government of India has set up the 'All India Handicrafts Board' in 1952 to study the problems confronting the handicrafts, to improve and develop production techniques, new designs and promote marketing in India and abroad[37].

With Industrialization becoming a National priority in 1960s and 1970s the government came to view Crafts as a 'Sun Set Industry' and focused mainly on welfare schemes rather than sectors capability to India's economic growth. Handicrafts come under the state list, each state has to setup its own handicraft policy. The State assists only those crafts and artisans who have high export potential. So the languishing crafts in turn suffer a lot, these artisans unable to reap the benefits of development schemes as they lack the assets and strong institutions supporting their cause.

The biggest problem while implementing the development schemes is the lack of proper knowledge on handicraft units and number of artisans. In 1993, DC(H) planned to conduct all Indian census of handicraft artisans and the task was given to NCAER New Delhi, which gave its survey report in 1995-96, indicating47.61 lakh artisans. However, from 11th five year plan (2007-2012), the central government had planned to conduct complete census of Handicraft artisans in the country over five year's period covering 20% districts every year.

As per the 12th five year plan's Working Group report on Handicrafts, an estimated 63% of artisans are self-employed while 37% are wage earners[38].

Traditional knowledge and craft skills are passed down from one generation to another so that whole families and communities are engaged in production. An estimated 71% of artisans work as family units and 76% attribute their profession to the fact that they have learned the family skill[39]. The official figures count only head of the production unit and wage earners, leaving out 5 to 6 members of the family who are also dependent on crafts for sustenance, thus creating incomplete understanding of sector's size and importance.

In order to safeguard the Crafts, the Government of India has a cabinet Ministry of Textile, under the ministry there are two separate 'Development Commissioners' for Handicrafts and Handlooms. Apart from this there are different sixteen other Ministries, namely Ministry of Agro and Rural Industries, Ministry of Tribal Development, Ministry of Rural Development and Ministry of Women and Child Development etc., with Crafts in their purview. These Administrative bodies have often been pitted against each other on the issues of protecting the interest of their respective Crafts leading to inefficiencies and policy juggernauts[40].

In the 11th Five year plan, government of India has provided Rs.752 Crore for craft sector. Institutions like 'Council for Advancement of People's Action and Rural Technology' (CAPART), 'Khadi and Village Industries Commission' (KVIC), Small Industries Development Bank of India (SIDBI) and the National Bank for Agriculture and Rural Development (NABARD) have been involved in funding and implementing development works for Artisans in the following areas.

Various *welfare schemes* such as *'Rajiv Gandhi Shilpi Swasthya Bima Yojana'* and *'Janasree Bima Yojana'* for handicraft artisans, which provides health and life insurance for the age group 18 – 60yr along with three dependent in association with LIC of India.

Establishment of *'Dilli Hatt'* an open-air Craft bazar in the National capital modeled on traditional village market, where artisans all over the country can rent space and display their products for two weeks at a stretch. Development Commissioners for Handicraft and Handloom run a number of emporiums as retail outlets for Crafts of different regions across the country, providing *market linkages* and access to consumers.

For sustainable development of Crafts through the participation of the artisans, government has made *capacity building* efforts like, Artisan Credit Card Scheme, *Baba Saheb Ambedkar Hastshilp Vikas Yojana* which are generally led by DC(H) and Handloom. Efforts include *skill development, technological intervention, design and marketing support.* Apart from this, Ministry of Textiles recognizes the work of several master craft people through distribution of *National Awards*.

(ii) Private Sector initiatives

Private sector conducts 95% Craft production through some private enterprise. Private involvement in Craft sector can be classified into four types

(a). Traditional Intermediaries

Master Craftsmen, Traders and Exporters who aggregate production provide market linkages offering finance to Artisans. Mostly, these relationships have been exploitative to the Artisans.

(b). Design Entrepreneur

These include high-end fashion houses that have imbedded traditional crafts in their collections by working closely with master craftsmen to create product offerings for high-end domestic and international markets. However, they never place Artisans at the center of their enterprises but rather integrate Crafts into their work.

(c). Mainstream Retail

A few retailers such as *FabIndia, Anokhi and Contemporary Arts and Crafts (CAC)*have played an important role in keeping Crafts relevant and linked to contemporary consumers. They work closely with Artisans ensuring them as equal stakeholders in the business. With well-organized supply chains, focus on profitability they provide the consumers with quality products of Urban taste than the government run emporiums.

(d). Social business

Social businesses offers access to quality inputs, equipment financing and training to the Artisans. Post-production, they improve market linkages, storage, transport and retail outlets. These ventures (namely, Ransutra and Industree) have the ability to raise capital from Artisans in the form of shares, as well as external investors as Capital funds and Corporates (Avishkar, Grassroots Business Fund and Villgro etc.,).

(iii) Non-profit interventions

These have been the strongest supporters of the Craft Industry both in terms of livelihood, promotion as well as cultural preservation. In 1960s and 1970s, when the government has shifted its economic priority from Craft Industry to Industrialization, a gap was created for supporting and financing the Craft sector. A number of non-profits were established in 1970s and 1980s to fill this gap and enhance the sustainability of Artisans. These non-profits run with the help of volunteers and were able to grow and thrive under a strong leader with clear vision for the sector. Most of the non-profits in Crafts are registered as Trusts, Societies or companies under Section-25. They are mainly of two types based on the scope of their work,

Producer group-These groups directly work at grassroots level, organizing craft producers into collectives to realize various economies of scale in financing, marketing and product development. Some of these groups are *URMUL, Kala Raksha and SEWA Ahmedabad etc.*

Apex Organizations – These groups focus on enhancing the sector by providing services ranging from design interventions to market linkages for a group of producers (who typically serve as a part of their membership base). These groups vary in scale of their outreach from National to State to Local levels. They also act as bridge between the Artisans and Government bodies by channeling information regarding government schemes, influencing government spending. Some of the prominent examples are *Dastkar, AIACA, Dastkar Hatt Samiti and Sasha.*

Non-profits are most effective at working with Artisans, building capacity and helping the Artisans develop skills due to their strong field knowledge of value chain. The failure of many Non-profits is due to their focus on creating linkages to market rather than creating market outlets themselves.

However, in-spite of significant contributions by Government, Private sector and Non-profits to the Artisan sector, the impact remained limited and they have not been able to prevent downward slide of the Indian Artisan Sector, since they acted in isolation from each other.

Current status of Government Initiatives

The following various comprehensive welfare Schemes, for *Handloom Weavers* of this country, have been offered by the Government of India[41].

i. Health Insurance Scheme(HIS)

The Health Insurance Scheme (HIS) aims to enable the weaver community to access healthcare facilities. HIS was implemented up to 30.9.2014 by Office of the Development Commissioner for Handlooms and now the scheme is implemented on Rashtriya Swasthya Bima Yojana (RSBY) platform by Ministry of Labour & Employment (MoLE) with enhanced benefits of Rs.37,500/- (Rs.7,500/- and Rs.30,000/- for OP & IP treatment respectively) for a family of five members.

ii. Mahatma Gandhi Bunkar Bima Yojana (MGBBY)

The Mahatma Gandhi Bunkar Bima Yojana aims to provide insurance cover to the handloom weavers in the case of natural death (Rs.60,000/-, accidental death (Rs.1,50,000/-), total disability (Rs.1,50,000/-) and partial disability(Rs.75,000/-). In addition, scholarship of Rs.300/- per quarter per child is available to students studying in IX to XII standard or for a maximum period of four years, whichever event occurs earlier. The Benefit is restricted to two children of the member covered. Under the scheme, funds are released directly to the implementing agency and not to any state. However, details of funds allocated, financial assistance provided, funds utilized during last three years are as under:-

Table – 1(i) Details of funds allocated and funds utilized during last three years

Year	*Funds Allocated*	*Financial assistance provided (GOI share)*	*(Rs. In crore) Funds utilised*
2011-12	104.50	68.22	68.22
2012-13	150.00	127.03	127.03
2013-14	95.00	66.24	66.24
2014-15	85.00	29.51 (till date)	25.26 (till date)

Source: Ministry of State (Independent Charge) in the Ministry of Textiles, reply over unstarred question No. 1714, in the Loka Sabha on 05.03.2015

Apart from this, *Health Insurance Scheme(HIS)* and *Mahatma Gandhi Bunkar Bima Yojana (MGBBY)* have been availed by 16,443 and 24,148 weavers hailing from newly evolved state of Telangana respectively as on up to 30.11.2014.

The Office of Development Commissioner (Handicrafts) has been offering following six prominent schemes namely,

(i) Baba Sahab Ambedkar Hastshilp Vikas Yojna

With the advent of Globalization, community empowerment programme for handicrafts sector/ cooperative / SHGs is a must to empower the artisans by making them active entrepreneurs-cum-primary stake holders of development and bringing them to a visible platform so as to enhance their operational efficiency and competitiveness to face the new challenges and make them viable and self-supporting economic entity.

(ii) Design & Technology up-gradation scheme

(iii) Marketing Support & Services Scheme

(iv) Human Resources Development Scheme

(v) Handicrafts Artisan comprehensive Welfare Scheme

(vi) Research & Development Scheme

Research and Development Scheme is a central sector scheme introduced in the year 1956-57 to generate feedback on Economic, Social, aesthetic and promotional aspects of various crafts and artisans in the handicrafts sector.

In order to avail these welfare schemes, the Artisan need to be registered, the registration of artisans is done by the respective marketing service centres and issue an ID card.

Table 1(ii)- Scheme-Wise Funds Released Under Handicrafts Schemes in Erstwhile Andhra Pradesh State

During 2012-13								
								Rs.in lakhs
SI. No.	State	AHVY	Design	MSS	HRD	welfare	R&D	Total
1	Andhra Pradesh	99.9	28.50	144.67	40.40	--	4.86	318.33

Source : Reply for starred question 166 in Loksabha by Ministry of Textiles.

Telangana State Scenario – towards Craft Sector

The State of Telangana has a number of internationally recognized forms of traditional arts and handicrafts. These are handicrafts like Nirmal Paintings, Dokra metal work, Bidri ware, Pembarthy Brass ware as well as textiles like Pochampally, Ikat, Gadwal saris and Warangal carpets. A number of artisans and craft-persons continue to live on the production of these arts and handicrafts, but there income levels are declining. To improve the productivity and incomes in this sector, the Government of Telangana intends to take a number of actions, including:

- Identification and documentation of arts and crafts
- Cluster approach for specific arts and crafts
- Technology upgrading and design support centers
- Skill up gradation and quality improvement
- Common facility centers
- IP and GI registration support
- Niche product development
- Marketing assistance and Marketing events participation

This program will be implemented under the *Telangana State Handicrafts and Artisans Revival with Technology* (*T-HART)* program. *Telangana Power-loom Weavers Loan Waiver Scheme G.O Ms.No.7, Dated 12.01.2015* is released by the DH&T and AEPs (I/C), Telangana State, Hyderabad, Lr.No.386/2014-P, Dt. 08.07.2014.

The Order reads as,

"In the reference read above, the Director of Handlooms & Textiles and Apparel Export Parks, Telangana State, Hyderabad has stated that there are (49,112) power-looms in Telangana State, out of which the majority of (38,000) power-looms are working alone in Siricilla Town. Due to insufficient earnings and fluctuations in the market, the power-loom weavers have become defaulters to the Banks. They are unable to pay back their Bank Loans taken for establishment of Power-loom Industry due to their meagre income generated out of income on power-loom weaving. The individuals have taken loans from different banks and which have become overdue/NPA. An amount of Rs.1586.10 lakhs is outstanding as on 31.03.2014 by 1325 number of individual power-loom weavers who took loans from various Banks.

Government, after careful examination of the proposal of Director of Handlooms & Textiles and Apparel Export Parks, Telangana State, Hyderabad, hereby decide to waive off the Bank/State Finance Corporation/ Co-Operative Bank loans of Rs.565.06 lakhs to the Power-loom Weavers, restricting the waiver upto Rs.1.00 lakh, in the State duly verifying the genuineness and thorough verification of the claims by the Director of Handlooms and Textiles and Apparel Export Parks, Telangana State, Hyderabad".

1.5 Evolution of Artisans

1.5.1 Potters

Kumhar (kummari, kumbharaa, Kubhara, kumar, kumor, kubar) is a caste or community in India. Kumhar literally means potter in Indian language [42]. Kumhars derive their name from the Sanskrit word *Kumbharkar* meaning *earthen-pot maker* [43]. Mythologically there is an opinion that because of their traditional creative skill of pottery, they are regarded as "Prajapathi" [44].

Potter is a community which is associated with human civilization itself, they must have been the first artisan to exist in India.

Vedic Pottery

Whilhelm Rau (1972) has examined the references to Pottery in *Vedic* texts like Black *Yajurveda* and *Taittiriya Samhita*, according to his study, Vedic pottery was handmade and unpainted[45]. Pottery in Indian subcontinent has remained as one of the most substantial and iconic elements of regional art. With time, Indian pottery went into evolution and a number of distinct styles emerged out from simple art of molding clay.

Indus Valley Civilization

Origin of pottery in India is traced back to Neolithic era with coarse handmade pottery comprising bowls, jars, vessels in various colors like red, orange, brown, black and cream. Beginning of Indian pottery is with Indus Valley civilization.

Pottery being carried out in two ways i.e., handmade and Wheel made[46]. *Harappan* and *Mohenjodaro* cultures heralded the age of wheel made pottery characterized by well-burnt black painted red wares.

Painted Grey Ware

During first millennium of BC, painted grey ware was found in parts of North India and the *Gangetic plain*. Decorated pottery became significant in the S*unga*, *Kushan* and *Gupta* periods[47].

Islamic Period

Glazed pottery started in 12th century A.D., when Muslim rulers encouraged potters from Iran and elsewhere to settle in India, this resulted in Glazed pottery of Persian models with Indian designs, which were found in Gujarat and Maharastra dating back to the period of Sultanate.

Over time India's simple style of molding clay went into an evolution and a number of distinct styles emerged from this simple style. Pottery in Indian villages presents a magnificent amalgamation of concept, design and execution apart from maintaining the cultural heritage of the country. There are mainly two types of Pottery found in Indian villages namely the unglazed pottery and glazed pottery. There are three different styles in unglazed pottery namely the *paper-thin, scrafito* and *high polished. Black pottery* is also another form of unglazed pottery in Indian villages which resembles the Harappan pottery style.

In *paper thin* pottery, the biscuit coloured pottery is decorated with carved patterns, which is produced in Kutch, Kanpur and Alwar in India.

In *Scrafito* technique of pottery, the pot is polished and painted red and white strips along with intricate patterns, while the outline is incised. The third is highly polished pottery, which is given strong, deeply incised, stylized patterns of arabesques. Unglazed pottery is practiced throughout the country, with each region having its own specialty.

Glazed pottery

The era of glazed pottery started in 12th century by the encouragement of Muslim rulers. It is practiced only in selected regions of the country, which contains a white background and blue and green patterns, which is commonly found in Delhi, Amritsar, Jaipur, Khurja in Uttar Pradesh, Karigars in Tamilnadu. Blue pottery of Delhi, Khurja and Jaipur is also glazed pottery.

Terracotta

Terracotta is yet another well-known and common style of pottery found in India. Women of Bihar, Bengal and Gujarat prepare clay figures to propitiate their Gods and Goddesses during festivals. *Moela* in Rajasthan has its own distinct styles of pottery in which local deities are created with molded clay on a flat surface, which are then fired and painted in bright colours.

The *Chittoor* area of Andhra Pradesh is well-known for its domestic 'Terracotta' or baked earth items. The villages of Tamilnadu are also quite famous for the terracotta figures of the Ayanar Deity. Huge figures found as standing guard at the entrances of the villages protecting the insiders of the village from evil spirits are terracotta. Utilitarian and home decoration items are made in Chota Nagpur, Aravallis, Orissa etc.

Apart from unglazed and glazed pottery, there are some other types of pottery produced in Indian villages. The major types of Pottery in Indian villages include the common earthen ware, Kullar (cup like container) lamps for Diwali toys for Dussehera, pots for seeding at Makara sankranthi, painted pots for marriages etc.

Karigari pottery is a type of pottery in Indian villages which is made with special attention by putting intricate designs on it. Decorative animal figures tea sets, ashtrays flower vases paper weights etc., are some examples of *Karigari* pottery.

Kagzi pottery

The pots are created with a technique to facilitate air circulation which helps to keep the water inside them cooler. This double wall impact in them is their unique quality. Alwar of Rajasthan is famous for Kagzi pottery i.e., making thin walled pottery containers.

Papier Machse Pottery

Papier Machse pottery is made with mashed paper pulp mixed with rice flour paste and copper sulphate. The mixture is covered with a thin paper and polished with bright colours. A golden shimmer is always present in this craft. So, we can find numerous types of pottery work in India in contemporary Age.

Hence, the potters supplied a range of vessels for all house-hold purpose like cooking utensils, *chulas*, *big huge containers* for storing grains, for storing water they supplied *pots, ranjans.* They also made vases for flowering plants which were used in palaces for decorating gardens etc., they made tiles for housing roofs. They supplied Diyas for Deepavali. So there was plenty of work for them and whole village communities (other than potters) depended on them for all these products. The potter community was leading a prosperous life during medieval period. They had a self-sufficient and a peaceful respectable life.

Pottery in Indian villages is hereditary Caste-based occupation. Almost every village in south India consists of potter communities, who are engaged in creating beautiful pieces of pottery which contain variety of household utensils and other objects of utility. Each potter has their own customers for whom they have to provide the pots for performing traditional rituals and the relation is continued for generations. Still in rural villages, we find potters having their own clients (i.e., 60 to 100 households) of nearby villages to whom they supply pots for performing Hindu traditional rituals during marriages, festivals,gruhapravesham and to perform last rites of dead etc.

The main tools utilized by these potters are convex stone, flat mallet and convention wheel. Indian states specialize in the production of wide variety of contemporary pottery works. World statistics revealed that India is the largest manufacturer and exporter of innumerable pottery handicrafts amongst the south Asian countries. Uttar Pradesh is one of the most significant contributors to the contemporary pottery Industry of India as several regions of the state export excellent pottery crafts to other nations.

India among the several other developing countries of Asia is considered as one of the first Asian Countries to manufacture as well as export products of pottery. The important markets for the pottery products are USA, Mexico, Hon Kong, Japan, Germany, Italy and France. However, the share of Global market of India in pottery is believed to less than 1%. The yearly production of pottery products in Khurja units of Uttar Pradesh is around 85 Crore of which 20% is exported to the international market.

The pottery industry, national level in general and Telangana region in particular, over the years has bravely battled several hindrances and still struggling to emerge in market. This profit earning industry in India is without any application of modern technical support most of their technologies are outdated and are inefficient, which failed this important industry to taste success in meeting the present market demands. In order to improve the overall condition of Indian pottery Industry (Telangana state in particular) it is important to identify the requirements of manufacturing centers, technological developments, making the local potters of rural Telangana region at grass root level aware of the modern trends of pottery market. Proper review of the industry, developing strong market linkages, value chain, analyzing the need, gap and formulating proper plans with will is very much important[48].

1.5.2 Weavers

The origin of Indian textiles can be traced back to the Indus Valley Civilization, excavations at Harappa and Mohenjo-Daro have unearthed house hold items like needles made of bone and spindles made of wood of around 3000BC, amply suggests that home-spun cotton was used to make garments.

Even Rig Veda and epics of the Mahabharata and the Ramayana dwell up on the craft weaving at length. These weavers were true masters of their craft, legend even refers to the fabulous semi-transparent sari worn by Amrapali a famous Courtesan.

India had numerous trade links with outside world; Indian textiles were very popular in Rome, Egypt and China. India was famous for its *Silk, Muslin and Chintz cotton.* In ancient and Medieval India, the textiles Industries were politically controlled by the then rulers. Differentiation was made between the rural textiles woven for masses, those made in State Workshops for royalty and best workmen ship for ritual hangings of temples.

Silk fabrics from South India were exported to Indonesia during 1300 AD. Dutch, French, Portuguese and British were fighting among themselves to have a big share of trade in Silk and Cotton fabrics with India. Such was the glory and fame of India Textiles around the world.

The intervention of Muslim rule in India (1200 AD to 1760 AD) brought new designs and styles like *Motifs, Dacca Muslins, Nakshas etc.* Changes in designs during the reign of various kings resulted in the development of weaving techniques and skills which not only enhanced the fabric with unique designs of *Zari, Silver, Gold brocades* intense *Meenakari* works, *Jamdani,* but also imbibed the culture in the craft leading to a unique cultural heritage.

During the British rule the East India Company exploited the India weavers by forcing them to sell the cloth at lesser prices than the market prices. The advent of Industrialization and invention of *Spinning mills*, further exploited the weavers. Discriminatory Fiscal and Social policies (levying heavy duty on Indian exports, cheap and qualitative machine made foreign goods, artificial scarcity of yarn etc.,) of the British slowly but surely paralyzed the hereditary hand-weaving industry. The English Governor General Bentinck reported in 1834 AD that "The misery hardly finds parallel in the history of Commerce, the bones of the cotton weavers are bleaching the plains of India".

The establishment of spinning and weaving mills in India, since 1854, compelled the native handloom weavers to depend on the mills spun yarn for raw material. During the India's Independence Struggle, *The Swadeshi Movement* seemed to help the handloom weavers, but in fact the Swadeshi ideology never singled out the weaver for a particular preference. In its campaign against foreign yarn and campaign for Indian mill cloth harmed the indigenous handloom weaver who consumed a lot of foreign yarn to compete with the mills.

Trade depressions of 1929-1930 further, paralyzed the handloom industry in India. Artificial scarcity of raw material created by middle man like *Mahajans, Master weavers, Yarn dealers etc.,* resulted in high cost of raw material which severely crippled handlooms[49].

Realizing the significance and suitability of Co-operatives for handloom weaving in India, Mr. *F. D. Harvell* first mooted the idea of forming "*Weavers' Co-operatives*" in 1907. The Royal Commission on Agriculture which visited India in 1928 AD observed that, "For survival of village industries in the fast increasing competition, it is essential that they are to be developed on a Co-operative basis", which resulted in the formation of the 'Co-operative planning committee' 1945, 'The Industrial Policy

Resolution of Govt. of India' 1948, 'The Village and Small Scale Industries Committee' 1955, 'Industrial Policy resolution' 1956, in post-independent India.

Organization of Handloom

The way handloom weavers operate is not uniform all over the state working in different modes and methods. The organization of Handloom weavers can be brought under three categories. They are

1. Co-operatives
2. Master weavers
3. Individual / Independent weavers

1. Co-operatives

Co-operatives can be *Primary weavers Co-operative Societies* and *Industrial weaving cooperative societies.*

(a) Primary Weaver's Cooperative Societies

These societies are formed with the purpose of making weavers involved in handloom weaving. Each society has a share-capital subscribed both by the weaver members and by the government. Weavers with looms can enroll themselves as members of society by paying share-capital, with one loom one to three members from the same family are given admission as members.

The main activity of the Primary Weavers Co-operative Society (PWCS) is to procure yarn (either from co-optex go-down or from other sources through NHDC with the permission of the Assistant director of Handlooms) and supply this yarn to the weavers and send finished fabric to the co-optex showrooms. Weaving takes place at the residence of the weavers where the weavers have their own looms. The society does not arrange for looms or other accessories required for weaving except supplying yarn. Weavers cooperatives are operated by paid staff officers (also known as "Handloom Officers") from the office of the Assistant Director of Handlooms.

(b) Industrial Weaver's Co-operative Societies

In these co-operative societies, the society owns and manages looms and accessories in common shed where the member weavers are expected to work. The society arranges for yarn and other raw materials required. The Society approves the plan of production (type of fabric to be weaved) based on the requirements accessed at the open market or as order placed by the co-optex or as desired by deemed exporters.

All the members work in a common shed and prepare goods as approved by the society. Each member is paid in proportion to the work done by him/her in the shed (piece-rate system). The society enrolls one or two members from one family. The members become eligible to obtain all government schemes meant for weavers, including insurance housing and stipend for children's education etc.

2. Master Weavers

They do not necessarily weave cloth; on the contrary they are owner-operators. There are two types of *Master Weavers.*

(a) Master weavers who do not own looms at all but have contacts with traders, from whom they procure orders and purchase yarn in bulk quantities from private spinning mills at competitive prices and get it weaved by the weavers who own looms at their homes by supplying them yarn raw materials. After a time period they receive the finished product, wages are paid for the quantity produced.

(b) Master Weaver installs a few looms in a shed for which he is the owner. The number of looms a master weaver owns ranges from 10 to 50. They hire weavers to fulfill the order they receive from a trader of cloth. This is not only the dominant sector but also a very profitable sector with 40% of weaving community working under them.

It is in this form the weaving sector seems to flourish in the globalized era, this form of transformation to a large extent has resulted in reduced status of the indigenous weaver from being an owner to a worker.

3. Individual or Independent Owners

This is the smallest group in the handloom industry. An independent weaver is one who weaves the cloth himself or by the members of his family. He owns loom / looms and purchases the raw material himself the finished products are sold in the market by his own effort. Sometimes they procure orders from traders and weave for them, and are paid by piece rate system. Only few percent of weavers come under this category.

Duo-weavers

They are the members of the co-operative who are not completely dependent on societies alone. They weave for the society only when the society supplies them yarn, when the society does not supply the yarn, they have some master weavers for whom they weave. This helps these weavers to tackle unemployment problem when the society faces problems like accumulated stock or scarcity of yarn etc.

The number of weavers working under each master weaver is not fixed at any point of time. This is because they keep shifting between master weavers and the cooperatives. Master weavers assume significance from the angle of dependency of the families of individual weavers on them. The relationship between the master weavers and the individual weavers is sort of symbiotic. The master weavers need the individual weavers to carry out the orders they get from dealers / traders. The individual weavers get festive advance, bonus etc. from master weavers which makes them keep working for them.

However, the individual weavers either working for the master weaver or for cooperatives is working by chance and not by choice.

Handloom markets

The cooperatives should supply 75% of their product to Co-optex, only the remaining 25% could go for open market as per the standing instructions of the government. Co-optex usually delays payments to co-operatives, even government also delays clearing rebate claims. These two realities i.e., payment due by Co-optex and rebate due by state government, are leading the weavers co-operatives into desperation. This discontent made the weavers to keep their names in co-operatives only to obtain government benefits by occasionally working in co-operatives; otherwise they work for private master weavers or for the traders.

The Handloom export depends on the 'deemed export system' only. These deemed exporters are private investors who are long time traders (players) in textile business. They have very clear strategy of dealing with weavers and with buyers. They work as middlemen without letting the producer know the buyer. This system has advantages along with risk factors.

Advantages

(i) The deemed exporter "supplies the yarn" in the quality the buyer wants it, which avoids cash credit facility requirement for weaver to buy raw material.

(ii) The deemed exporter "decides which items are to be produced", relieving the weaver from market worry.

(iii) No chance of deemed exporters delaying payment to weavers. They send Demand Drafts within a fortnight time.

(iv) Payments of wages are comparatively better.

(v) There is no problem of marketing.

Limitations

(i) The quality of work and finishing have to match 100% with given prescription, else exporters reject the produce.

(ii) An order placed should be delivered on time. Delay not accepted, may affect the next order.

(iii) As more and more weavers approach the "Deemed exporters" for orders leading to declining trend in wage payments year after year.

(iv) Competition in the international market for Indian textile in foreign too intense resulted in cost-cut by the deemed exporter reflecting in wages paid to weavers.

1.5.3 Blacksmiths

Lohar (lohara) is a sub-caste among Hindus and Sikhs and a clan among Muslims in Northern India, Northern Pakistan and Nepal[50,51]. In India Lohars are also known as *Vishwakarma*, Sharma or Panchals. Muslim Lohar in North India called as Saifi. Lahore of Pakistan was once called Loharpur, the city of Lohar dynasty. The Vishawakarma (orVisvakarma) community refer themselves as viswabrahmin and is sometimes described as a caste. The community comprises five sub-groups – carpenters; blacksmiths, bell metal workers, goldsmiths and stone masons.

They believe, they are descendants of Vishwa karma a Hindu deity. They worship various forms of this deity and follow five Vedas i.e., Rig-Vedas, YajurVeda, Sama Veda, Atharva Veda and Pranava Veda[52].

Position in Society

They claimed a higher status for many years and believe that their work is superior to manual labour because it requires artistic, scientific skill along with hand labour. According to *George Varghese* it is fragmented, incoherent community suffering from internal differences of opinion[53].

Edavva Somanathan a member of community and its only historian in the written work argues that artisanal groups were a part of the Indus valley civilization, pre-dating the arrival of Brahmins and their caste-based divisionof society. He claims remarkable achievements are evidenced in both arts and sciences during that egalitarian pre-Brahmin era including construction of airplanes.

Their claim of Brahmin status is not generally accepted outside the community, despite of some high-caste traits, such as wearing sacred thread, Brahmanization of their rituals. They have been included in the list of other backward classes[54].

The Devine Draftsman

According to Hindu mythology, Vishwakarma is the presiding deity of all craftsmen and architects. Son of Brahma, he is the divine draftsman of the whole universe and official builder of all God's palaces. Vishwakarma is also the designer of all flying chariots of gods and their weapons.

The Mahabharata describes him as "lord of all arts, executor of thousand handicrafts the most eminent of all artisans, the fashioner of all ornaments. Hindus widely regard Vishwakarma as the god of architecture and engineering, and 16th or 17th September every year is celebrated as Vishwakarma puja – a resolution time for workers and craftsmen to increase productivity and gain divine inspiration for creating novel product. The ritual is performed in the premises of production.

Vishwakarma according to Hindu mythology built "Sone ki Lanka" in "Treta Yuga" the city of Dwarca in "Dwapar Yuga", and Hastinapur and Indraprastha in "*Kali Yuga*".

A Magic Material

No substance has been so important as metal in the history of man's control of his environment. Advances in agriculture, warfare, transport, even cookery are impossible without metal. Nature attracts man into the adventure of metallurgy by gifting him first with Gold. It can be easily shaped by hammering; this malleability makes it useless for practical purposes except for jewelry (surviving gold jewelry 3000BC form Egypt).

The second metal to be discovered from nature in pure form was Copper. This resulted in Copper Age from 6000 BC, a few Neolithic communities began hammering copper into crude knives and sickles. The use of fire thus made possible two significant steps in the development of metallurgy.

1. The casting of metal by pouring it into prepared molds
2. The smelting of mineral ores to extract metal.

This led inevitably to the development of mining (the first miners from 4000BC).

Sometimes the ores of Copper and Tin are found together, casting of which accidently led to the invention of new metal bronze in metallurgy. This resulted in the civilization of Bronze Age (from 3000 BC). Bronze metal gave sharp edges than copper with more longevity, which were found in Indus Valley Civilization about 2500 BC. It was the rulers who used Bronze as a luxury for themselves or as a weapon for their armies[55].

The Age of Iron (from 1500 BC)

The next metal to be discovered was Iron, which resulted in Iron Age. The melting point of iron was too high for primitive furnaces to extract it in pure form, from its ores. It was turned to a useful method by repeated heating and hammering until impurities were literally forced out. It was heated and hammered but never melted because the melting point of Iron (1528 ^{0}C) too high for primitive furnaces, which could reach only 1300^{0}C adequate for Copper (melts at 1083 ^{0}C). However Chinese developed a furnace hot enough to melt iron enable to produce world; first *Cast Iron* in 513 BC.

By 11th century BC it was discovered that if Iron reheated in a furnace with Charcoal (containing Carbon), some of the carbon is transfer to the Iron, which hardens the metal, the effect was considerably greater if this hot metal was repeatedly reduced in temperature by quenching it in water. The new material was steel. It was like softer Iron with finer edge, capable of being groomed to sharpness, this made Steel to replace Bronze weapons.

Perhaps as early as 300 BCE, although certainly by 200CE high quality steel was being produced in Southern India by what Europeans would later call – Crucible technique. In this technique high-purity wrought Iron and charcoal, were heated until the iron melted and absorbed the carbon. The resulting high Carbon Steel called *Fulad* in Arabic and *Wootz* by later Europeans was exported throughout much of Asia and Europe.

The first Crucible steel was the *Wootz* Steel that originated in India before the beginning of Common Era[56]. *Wootz* steel was widely exported and traded throughout ancient Europe, China and Arab world and became famous in the Middle East as "Damascus Steel". Archeological evidences suggest that this manufacturing process existed in Southern India much before Christian Era[57,58].

At that time the fame of India's *Wootz* steel was well recognized around the world. The high status of Indian steel could be reflected by the following facts.

(i) It was accepted as precious gift by *Alexander* from India.

(ii) *King Porus* took thirty pounds of this steel from *Alexander* as a gift.

(iii) According to Arabic sources Prophet Mohammad is also said to have had a Sword made of *Hindwani Steel.*

The world's first Iron pillar was the "*Iron Pillar of Delhi*", erected at the times of *Chandragupta II Vikramaditya* (375-413)[59]. This Iron Pillar of victory is 23.08 foot tall and 16 inches in diameter at the base weighing 6.3 tons. This Delhi *Iron Pillar* with no cover over it has withstood the vagaries of weather for 1700 years continuously with no sign of rusting so far, which has attracted the attention of archeologists and metallurgists and has been called as "a testament of skill of ancient Indian blacksmiths" because of its high resistance to corrosion. Tipu sultan's sword known for its toughness due to high Carbon content, was auctioned for £ 502,500 at *Sotheby's auction* in 2012 in London. A team of researchers of National Institute for Advanced Studies (NIAS), Bangalore and UK's Exeter University tried to trace the origin of metal.To their utter surprise they found out that the sword was made by Blacksmiths of Telangana who lived between present Nizamabad and Hyderabad.

Statues of *Nataraja* and *Vishnu* were caste during the reign of the imperial *Chola dynasty* (200-1279) in the 19th century[60]. The casting involved a mixture of five metals: Copper, *Zinc, Tin, Gold and Silver*[61].The fame of Indian *Wootz* steel could be traced in the words of *Arab Edrisi* (12th Century), "The Hindus excelled in the manufacture of Iron and it is impossible to find anything to surpass the edge from Hindwani or Indian Steel".

The swords manufactured in Indian workshops find written mention in the works of *Mohammad al-Idrisi* (flourished in 1154)[62]. Indian blades made of Damascus steel found their way into Persia[63], European scholars – during the 14th century studied Indian casting and metallurgy technology[64].

Indian metallurgy under the Mughal emperor *Akbar* (Reign: 1556-1607) produced excellent small fire arms[65]. The "*Ain-i-Akbari*" by *Abul Fazal* is major work on the arsenal making during Akbar's time, which describes about personal swords of Akbar. *Gommans* (2002) holds that Mughal handguns were stronger and more accurate than their European counterparts. During mid-17th century Indian *Wootz* was so famous and was exported to all over the world and contributed to rich traditions of Indian armory too.

In 16th and 17th century, many trading firms from the *Dutch*, the *French*, and the *British East India* Company came to India to trade and soon gained political control. In their effort of gaining the political power, they were resisted by the native rulers like *Tipu Sultan, Rani of Jhansi, Rani Chennamma, and Shivaji etc.,* which made the British realize the strength and superior quality of Indian swords. During the reign of *Tipu Sultan* the art of metallurgy for fashioning rockets was mastered, which could reach 2.5 Km with fair degree of accuracy. Several Indian rockets were taken to Britain to understand and study the technology which was superior to their Western equivalents.

After the Indian *Sepoy mutiny* in 1857, the British ordered the destruction of all the *Wootz* swords. They developed a special machine to destroy the Damascus blades often the shearing blades of these machines were cut by the tough *Wootz* swords, and British then had to devise a protective measure for their shearing machines.

Though *Wootz* was such an important material in the history of metals much is not written about Indian *Wootz* steel by Indigenous people, but much has been written by travelers from *Italy, France* and *England.*

In the early decades of the 20th Century the fame of *Wootz Steel* began to decline. British colonization led to its near extinction. It was *J.N. Tata* who revived the dying steel Industry. His efforts led to the setting up of Tata Iron and Steel plant (earlier known as TISCO) in 1907 opened its plant at Jamshedpur in then Bihar, now in the state of Jharkhand[66]. Today's patent for *Ultra High Carbon Steel (UHCS)* in reality is influenced by an ancient technique which was developed in India many centuries ago rather than being a modern innovation. It used American Technology not British and became the leading Iron and Steel producer in India.

In the contemporary age, the skill of making *Wootz Steel* is completely lost in our country with no traces left behind except from the debris of crucibles scattered randomly over parts of South India, though rural Black-smithy is still being practiced quite widely all over India to make agricultural tools, ploughshares, utensils etc. With the advancement of Scientific Knowledge i.e., Quantum mechanics, Nano technology one can decipher more knowledge of ancient metals. Damascus steel is a result of a kind of *Nanotechnology,* when the size reduces to nanometer level, Quantum effect takes place. So scientists are making efforts to understand *Damascus steel* in modern times with these two techniques.

Blacksmiths – Telangana Scenario

Northern Telangana comprises the four districts of Adilabad, Nizamabad, Karimnagar and Warangal, bisected by the course of the Godavari River. In the past it was major centre of iron and steel production as recorded in historical accounts and field investigations in the 1980's by Thelma Lowe of Berkeley University.

In recent years the publication of *Dr S. Jaikishan* (2009) has brought the Archaeo-Metallurgical record of Telangana in general and Northern Telangana in particular. The blacksmiths of the Telangana region, like most of the blacksmith communities of south India, fall within the Viswakarma (the Hindu god of arts and crafts) caste group. The Viswakarma caste in the Telangana region consists of five distinct craft communities; blacksmiths, gold-smiths, bronze-smiths, carpenters and stonemasons or sculptors.

Although intermarriage is often practiced among the three metal craft communities, it is not altogether clear whether the matrimonial relations are encouraged with the non-metal craft groups (carpenters and stonemasons). Marriage outside the caste is not encouraged. The Viswakarma caste of the Telangana region, including the blacksmith community, wear sacred threads like the Brahmins and a sense of strong inter-caste competition with the Brahmins could be observed in the traditions and taboos of the blacksmith community.

The blacksmith communities frequently occur as close clusters within larger rural settlements, often not very far from the location of a slag or crucible heap. Spatially, their residences and workspaces are situated closer to the residential cluster of the agricultural community, who are their primary clients. The community is stratified according to seniority and is headed, in each village, by a body of elder blacksmiths (consisting generally of three or four senior smiths) who preside over communal meetings, which are generally held on every new moon evening and in the premises of the temple of their goddess, Mammayee. The elder blacksmiths are responsible for making all important decisions regarding community disputes, auspicious and inauspicious days and festivals.

In most cases their decisions are deemed as final and unquestionable. Women are strictly prohibited from participating in any aspect of blacksmithing and the cult of their goddess.

The business relationship between the farmers and blacksmiths were regulated through a long-standing tradition of oral contract, where the individual farmer agrees to pay a certain amount of grain (normally rice or pulses) to the blacksmith, who in turn has to make or mend as much agricultural equipment as the farmer asks from him. The payment comes in two instalments i.e., after two harvest seasons. This seemed to be a very well established tradition in most of the villages of the region. Apart from some villages which are closer to urban centres or highways, monetary transaction is not preferred. The system of two instalments is strictly followed even during a cash transaction with the farmers.

Blacksmiths, in global era, prefer to accept cash due to the wandering nature of their work. The blacksmiths manufacture tools exclusively to fulfil the needs of the immediate rural community. Mass production of the iron implements is not practiced and manufacture or repair is done only on request, probably due to the declining market of indigenously produced items in competition with industrialised products.

Consequently, all of them are primarily engaged in repair work rather than manufacture of new tools. Raw materials are generally procured from the market by the farmers, rather than the blacksmiths themselves, in the form of scrap industrial iron, commonly as lorry springs. Charcoal can be purchased from local markets but sometimes the blacksmiths prefer to make charcoal themselves from locally abundant teak wood.

Although the region is rich in ore, smelting is no longer practised and it appears that the knowledge of smelting technology is significantly lost, except in the memories of few elders.

Cultural Fest of Blacksmith - Mammayee Festival

The festival of the goddess Mammayee traditionally takes place in the last eleven days of the Telugu calendar, which normally falls in early March, which coincides with Telugu New Year's Day. However, due to poverty among the blacksmiths of this region, the festival celebrations are reduced to three days. One of the cult of goddess is at Ibrahimpatnam of Karimnagar district. On the first day of this festival the blacksmiths cease to work and donate some of their working tools to the nearby Mammayee temple. Only vegetarian food is cooked strictly within the Temple premises by

Fig. 1(i) The Mammayee goddess

Blacksmiths. Women are not allowed in the cult performances, the cult of Mammayee seems to be exclusively followed by the blacksmith community.

On the final day of the festival the blacksmiths gather in the temple before sunrise and prepare food offerings with *pulses, rice, maize, coconut and jaggery*. The final worship is conducted by the senior blacksmiths, with the senior-most of them acting as high priest, reciting mantras. After these rituals, the blacksmiths gather in the temple courtyard and help each other in tying the fresh, turmeric-dipped, sacred thread.

Finally, they tie sacred threads on their working implements, which appear to be extensions of a blacksmiths' body and rejuvenated through endowment of divine power and the blessings of the goddess. This is followed by the inauguration of the smithy in individual workspaces. This is done by hitting the anvil in three sets of five, first by the eldest family member followed by others according to age. Then, while the eldest smith is required to light the hearth and manufacture an agricultural implement, the next in line operates the fan bellows (hand-turned). Finally, the junior apprentices of the family carry the newly produced implements to the houses of the farmers, who, in turn, are required to offer rice, pulses, turmeric and garlic in exchange for the implements. Thus the long-standing relationship with the farming community is renewed through a ritual contract.

Extinction of *Jajmani system* and modernization of agriculture to a very large extent led to the migration of blacksmiths in search of livelihood. In this Globalized era, most of the blacksmiths who are still depending on same traditional caste occupation struggle for sustenance and have become nomads, so the significance of *Mammayee* festival is faded and most of the blacksmiths not even aware of their traditional fest.

Reference

1. Dube S.C., 1955, *Indian Village*, Foreword by Morris E. Opler, Ithaca: Cornell University Press.
2. Bailey, F. G., 1957, *Caste and the Economic Frotiers: A Village in Highland Orissa,* Manchester, Manchester University Press.
3. Lewis, Oscar., 1958, *Village Life in Northern India,* Illinois, University of Illionois Press.
4. Srinivas, M. N. 1959, *The Dominant Caste in Rampura,* American Anthropologist, NS, Vol. 61, No. 1, pp. 1-16.
5. Mehta, R.J., 1960, *The Handicrafts and Industrial Arts of India,* Published by Bombay: Taraporevala.
6. Abraham, T.M., 1964, *Handicrafts in India,* New Delhi: graphics Columbia.
7. Chattopadhyay, Kamaladevi, 1976, *The Glory of Indian Handicrafts,* New Delhi: India Book Company.
8. Pal, P. K., 1978, *Crafts and Craftsmen in Traditional India,* Kanak Publications, New Delhi.
9. Ranjan, Aditi and Ranjan, M. P. (Eds), 2007, *Handmade in India: Crafts of India,* co-published by COHANDS and Mapin Publishers Pvt. Ltd., National Institute of Design, Ahmedabad.
10. Liebl, Maureen and Roy, Tirthankar, 2003, *Handmade in India: A Preliminary Analysis of Crafts and Craft Production*, Economic and Political Weekly, Vol. 38, No. 51/52 (Dec 27, 2003-Jan. 2, 2004), pp. 5366-5376.
11. Sennett, Richard, *2008, The Craftsman,* Yale University Press.
12. Chadha, G.K., (1997), *Access of Rural Households to Non-farm employment: Trends, constraints and possibilities,* in G.K. Chedha and Alakh N Sharma (eds), Op Cit., pp 184-215.
13. Fisher, T., Mahajan, V., and Singha, A., (1997), The Forgotten Sector, Intermediate TechnologyPublications London, p 274.
14. Hezell, P.B.R., and Haggblade, S., *Rural Growth Linkages in India,* Indian Journal of Agricultural Economics, 46(4), pp 515-29.
15. Unni, J., (1998), *Non-Agricultural employment and poverty in rural India – A Review evidence,* Economic and Political Weekly, 33(13), pp. A36-A44.
16. Deshpande, S., and Deshpance, L., (1998), *Impact of Liberalisation on Labour Market in India, what Facts from NSSO's 50th Round Show?,*Economic and Political Weekly, 33(2), L31-40.

17. Shrivastava, A., Athavale, M.C., and Gupta, S.K., (1995), *Impact of Non-farm Employment on Income Generation in Similar farms: A case study in Two districts of M.P.,* Indian Journal of Agricultural Economics, 50(3), pp 448-449.
18. Saraf, D.N., 1982, *"Indian Craft"*, Vikas Publishing House.
19. Kamaladevi Chettopadyay, *Handicrafts of India,* 2nd edn, Indraprastha Press, New Delhi, 1985.
20. Aryan, S, *Craft of Himachal Pradesh,* Mapin Publishing Ahmedabad, India, 1993.
21. Sai Deepak, J., *Protection of Traditional Handicrafts under Indian Intellectual Property Rights,* Journal of Intellectual Property Rights, Vol. 13, May 2008, pp 197-207.
22. UNESCO, http://portal.unesco.org
23. Ministry of Textiles, Govt. of India, *Working Group report on Handicrafts for 12th Five year plan, 2011: Crafts Council of India,* Craft Economics and Impact Study: Stage-1 & Stage-2, 2011.
24. Jena P.K., *Orissan Handicrafts in the Age of Globalization: Threats and Opportunities,* in Mukherjee D, Indian Handlooms and Handicrafts : Issues and Experiences, 2009.
25. Doshi, S. L., and Jain P. C., *Rural Sociology*, Rawat Publications.
26. Heather L. Ross and Isabel V. Sawhill , *The family as Economic Unit,* The Wilson Quarterly / Winter 1977.
27. Asha Krishnakumar, *Caste and the Census*, Volume 17 - Issue 18, Sep. 02 - 15, 2000, Frontline, India's National Magazine, from the publishers of THE HINDU.
28. Yousuf Dhamee, 1996, *Adam Smith and Division of Labour,* The Victorian Web, www.victorianweb.org
29. Johnson L, *Legal Structures for community – owned enterprises,* presentation at LEAD Workshop, Ahmedabad, 2011.
30. AIACA and ACCESS Development Services, Artistic Textiles of Nagaland : Diagnostic Study and Business Development plan, www.aiacaonline.org
31. Liebl M, Roy T, *Handmade in India : Preliminary Analysis of Crafts Producers and Crafts Production,* World Bank, Published in Economic and Political Weekly, 2003.
32. India, Science and Technology, *S&T for Rural India and Inclusive growth 2008*, http://www.nistads.res.in
33. Ministry of Textiles, Govt. of India, *Working Group Report on Handicrafts for 12th five year plan,* 2011.
34. Subramanian, K. K., *An overview of the Handicrafts Industry,* In Subramanian K.K. (ed.), The Handicraft Industry in Kerala: Blending heritage with economics, Dannish Books, Delhi, 2006.
35. Stiglitz, J., *Globalization and its Discontents*, Penguin, New York , 2002.
36. Dasra,*Catalyst for Social Change,* Report on Crafts –January, 2013, p.15-25.
37. Upadhyay, M.N., *Handicrafts of India*, Swarajya Printing Works, Secunderabad, 1976.

38. Ministry of Textiles, Govt. of India, *Working Group Report on Handicraft for* 12th five year plan 2011.

39. Jaitly J, *Visvakarma's Children : Stories of India's Craft people*, 2001, Published by A K Mittal, Concept publishing company, New Delhi, ISBN: 81-7022 -895-6.

40. Planning Commission: Eleventh Five Year Plan, Ensuring Rural and urban Livelihoods, 2008, http://planningcommission.gov.in/plans/planrel/fiveyr/11th/11_v3/11v3_ch5.pdf

41. Lok SabhaUn-starred Question No. 1714, Answered on05.03.2015 on *Handloom Weavers Comprehensive Welfare Schemes* by Ministry of Textiles, Government of India.

42. Saraswati baaidyanath (1979), *Pottery-Making Cultures And Indian Civilization,* Abhinav Publications pp 46-47 ISBN 978-81-7017-091-4.

43. Mandal S.K. (1998), *Kumhar/Kumbhar,* In Singh, Kumar Suresh, *People of India: Rajastan,* Popular Prakahkashan pp. 565-566, ISBN 978-17154-769-2.

44. Bharati, Ke. Ara (2001), *Chamba Himalaya: Amazing Land, Unique Culture, Indus* Publishing p.178 ISBN 978-8-17387-125-2.

45. Edwin Bryant, *Quest for the Origins of Vedic Culture,* 2001: pp. 211-212.

46, http://www.culturalindia.net/indian-crafts/indian-pottery.html

47. Keshav Chandra Gupta , Progress and Prospects of Pottery industry in India : A case study of U.P. Mittal Publications, pp. 18 – ISBN 978-81-7099-051-2.

48. http://busines.mapsofindia.com/indiaindstry/pottery.html

49. Jawaharlal Nehru, *The Discovery of India,* Jawaharlal Nehru memorial fund, New Delhi, Oxford University Press, 1982, p. 298.

50. Bhattachan Krishan B. (2008), *Indigenous people & Miniorities of Nepal*, Nepal Federation of Indigenous Nationalities (NEFIN), p. 49.

51. Bhattarai, Hari Prasad (2004), "*Cultural Diversity and pluralism in Nepal : Emerging Issues and the Search for a New Pardigm",* Contributions to Nepalese Studies, p. 339.

52. "*Karnataka State Gazetteer: Belgaum",* printed by the Director of Print Stationery and Publications at the Govt. press.

53. Varghese K., George (2003), *"Globalization Traumas and new Social imaginary: Visvakarma Community of Kerala",* Economic and Political Weekly, 38(45).

54. Berger, Peter, Heidemann, Frank, *"The Modern Anthropology of India: Ethnography, Themes and Theory",* Routledge, p.128, ISBN: 9781134061112.

55. Srinivasan, Sharda and Srinivasa Rangnathan, (2004), *India's Legendry Wootz Steel,* Bangalore: Tata Steel, p. 146.

56. Srinivasan, S & Ranganathan, S., "*Wootz Steel : An Advanced material of the Ancient World,* Indian Institute of Sciences, Bangalore.

57. Srinivasan, S (1994), "*Wootz crucible steel : a nearly discovered production site in South India,* Institute of Archaeology, University College London, 5 : 45-61.

58. Srinivasan, S. & Griffiths, D., "*South Indian wootz : evidence for high-carbon steel from crucibles from a nearly identified site and preliminary comparisons with related finds*", Material issues in Art and Archaeology-V, Materials Research Society Symposium Proceedings Series, Vol. 462.

59. Balasubramaniam, R (2000), "*Delhi Iron Pillar: New Insights, Indian Institute of Advanced Studies,* ISBN-81-7305-223-9.

60. Mondal Biswanath (2004), "*Proceedings of the National Conference on Investment Casting : NCIC2003*", Allied Publishers, ISBN 81-7764—659-1.

61. *Ibid.*

62. Edgerton et.al., (2002), "*Indian and Oriental Arms and Armour*", Courier Dover Publications, ISBN-0-486—42229-1.

63. Prasad, P.C., (2003), "*Foreign Trade and Commerce in Ancient India*", Abhinav Publications, ISBN 81-7017-053-2.

64. *Ibid.*, ref. 156.

65. Gommans, Jos J.L., (2002), "*Mughal Warfare : Indian Frontiers and Highroads to Expire 1500- 1700*", Routledge, ISBN 0-415-23989-3.

66. "*India's legendary Wootz steel*", *Material Engineering division, IISc, Banglore.*

Chapter - 2

Theoretical Perspectives on Caste

The study is based on Indian caste occupations, traditions of sociology of caste, sociology of migration, occupational mobility, sociology of market, and concepts of urban sociology. Sociological discussion on caste in India has its beginnings in the middle of 19th century in the writings of travelers, missionaries and above all civil servants. The 'Sociology for India' has long ago established the futility of understanding caste and caste system in India only through the textual version of the *'Purusashukta'* origin[1], or only by relying on empirical ethnographic studies, and has come up with varying explanations of contextualizing caste.

"Caste cannot be abolished in India, and to attempt, it would be of one of the most hazardous operations that was ever performed in a political body. As a religious institution caste will die, as a social institution, it will live and improve". (*Max Muller* 1869:353).

Max Weber's "The Religion of India" originally published in 1921, was a particularly scholarly and persuasive argument that Hinduism and the caste system- supported by Hindu beliefs in rebirth, retribution, and reward for meritorious and sinful behaviour - would function as obstacles to modern capitalism and industry[2].

Gunnar Myrdal sees the caste system as an obstacle to economic and political modernization (*Myrdal* 1972:80,147,177). In contrast, others have found the caste system to be flexible and adaptive, most notably, the anthropologist, *Milton Singer* (1972, 1973) and the historical sociologist, *Barrington Moore, Jr.* (*Moore*, 1966: 334).

J.H. Hutton defines caste as "a collection of families or groups of families bearing a common name; claiming a common descent from a mythical ancestor, human or divine; professing to follow the same hereditary calling; and regarded by those who are competent to give an opinion as forming a single homogenous community". He goes on to add that the caste name is generally associated with a specific occupation and that a caste is almost invariably endogamous, but is further divided, as a rule, into a number of smaller circles each of which is endogamous[3].

A status segregation grown into caste differs in its structure from a mere 'ethnic' segregation; the caste structure transforms the horizontal and unconnected coexistences of ethnically segregated groups into a vertical social system of super-ordination and subordination ...ethnic coexistences condition a mutual repulsion and disdain but allow each ethnic community to consider its own honour as the highest one; the caste structure brings out a social subordination and an acknowledgement of 'more honour' in favour of privileged castes and status groups (*Gerth and Mills* 1946: 189)[4]

Gough views castes as "ranked birth-status groups which are usually endogamous and tend to be associated with an occupation". *Senart* (1930) has described caste as "a closed corporation, rigorously hereditary, bound with others (castes) by common occupation, and equipped with a council that rules its members by the sanction of certain penalties".

In structural terms, *Bougie* has explained castes as "hereditarily specialised and hierarchically arranged groups", while as a system, he has referred to its three characteristics: hierarchy, hereditary specialization, and repulsion.

Bailey and *Srinivas* have viewed castes as structures and have avoided the definition of caste. *Dutt*, describing caste system has referred to restrictions on marriage, eating and drinking, occupation, change in hereditary membership, and the hierarchical gradation of castes. Morris also believes that a short definition of caste is not satisfactory so it is more illuminating to talk in terms of the characteristics of caste" He describes caste system as "characterised by hereditary membership and endogamy and prescribing specific norms which regulate socialism interaction".

Ghurye has given features of the caste system. Besides, referring to hereditary membership, caste councils, hierarchy and endogamy as important features of the caste system, he also refers to the restrictions on feeding and social intercourse, lack of unrestricted choice of occupation, and civil and religious disabilities. D' Souza has referred to the definition of caste system as "the integration of the interacting and heterogeneous but internally homogeneous hereditary groups into a structure of status hierarchy".

Yogender Singh who holds authority on sociology of social stratification defines caste as a major form of stratification. He writes "Sociologists who look across the cultural view of caste have, right from the beginning, associate with an autonomous principal of stratification. The bases of which are institutionalized inequality, closure of social system in respect of social mobility, an elementary level of division of labour, legitimized on ritual bases of reciprocity, and emphasis on quality (ritual purity or racial purity) rather than performance. In other words Caste is associated with an autonomous form of cultural system of world view"[5].

According to *Yogender Singh*, Caste is a cultural phenomenon, and also a structural phenomenon. Caste as a structural phenomenon is a system of social organization, an institutionalized system of interaction among hierarchically-ranked hereditary groups for marriage, occupation, economic division of labour, enforcement of cultural norms and values by caste bodies and performance of rituals based on the principles of purity and pollution. The structural properties of caste namely endogamy, caste occupations and hierarchy have a direct bearing on social stratification. The cultural aspects on other hand are value-based.

Singh holds that structurally, the caste system simultaneously manifests two tendencies: one, segmental and other, organic. As a segmental reality, each caste or a sub-caste tends to articulate mutual repulsion, social distance and social inequality, but as an organic system, the caste segments are mutually interlinked by a principle of reciprocity through the *Jajmani system. Bailey* (1960) has referred to caste stratification as a 'closed organic stratification' in contra-distinction with the class principle which is based on 'segmentary stratification'. In the former, the social segments (castes or sub-castes) interact through cooperation and in the latter through competition.

K.L. Sharma provides an interesting social profile of the new caste which is fast emerging in our villages, "There are new castes not really in the hereditary/ascriptive sense of the term caste, but in terms of the emergence of new status groups taking precedence over the traditional upper and middle castes. Social mobility in the caste system has been a historical fact, and every new macro-economic and political development has affected the caste system. These changes in the caste system may be seen in the decline of Jajmani system and emergence of modern occupations and in the form of new dominant groups and families, decline of untouchability and the pollution-purity principle"[6].

A variety of stratification textbooks and studies of status hierarchies tend to classify caste as a form of stratification rooted in religion and universally accepted by the dominant as well as subordinate groups in the hierarchy *(Grusky, K.U. and Szelenyi 2008, Gould 2002)*[7,8].

Louis Dumont followed attributional approach to the study of Caste system, by emphasizing on the attributes of caste. He viewed caste as set of economic, political and kinship systems sustained by certain values which religious in nature. Caste is not a form of *stratification* but a special form of inequality for him. He says Indian society is divided into large number of hereditary groups distinguished from one another and connected together by three characteristics i.e.,

(i) Separation on the basis of rules of caste
(ii) Interdependence of work or division of labour by tradition, a profession from which their members can depart only within certain limits.
(iii) Hierarchy, which ranks the groups as relatively superior or inferior to one another.

He calls caste system as a system of "*ideas and values*" which is a "*formal comprehensible rational system*". His analysis is based on the principle of opposition of *pure and impure* which underlies hierarchy along with separation, meaning superiority of pure and inferiority of impure.[9]

In *'Homo Hierarchicus'* (1966), *Louis Dumont* presented: The Caste as a system of "*ideas and values*", as a religious ranking to classify things and beings according to their dignity. It is a traditional *'division of labour'* (*Jajmani system)* based on religious values rather than on economic logic. He viewed the only significant change that has taken place is the traditional interdependence of castes has been replaced by '*a universe of impenetrable blocks, self-sufficient, essential, identical and in competition with one another*', which he calls as the *'Substantializaton of Castes'*. For *Dumont*, any plausible explanation of caste has to be in terms of relations between castes. This relationality for him was further maintained and grasped only in terms of and in relation to encompassing set of religious values (i.e., which encompasses and that which is encompassed)[10].

The field view, in 1950's and 1960's, in the form of ethnographic monographs indeed enriched and complicated the coherent view of Indian society produced by the Indologists. Prior to 1950's and 1960's earlier colonial administrators, scholars, census officials, pioneering travel writers had already produced a great deal of empirical work which flew in the face of the uniformity and conformity that classical texts presented before the Indologists.

Dumontian theorization of caste as *essentialisation, eroticization, totalisation* (*Appadurai*1988: 41). *Dumont's* substantive disagreements with the existing literature on caste had something more to do than with his methodological instance on confluence of the '*book view*' and the '*field view*'. He positioned himself against,

(i) Treating the Indian caste system as merely an instance – if extreme at that social stratification.
(ii) Understanding particular castes as substantive entities at the expense of a defining focus on the relations that obtain among them.
(iii) Empiricism at the expense of a focus on an encompassing set of values.
(iv) Adopting a perspective of individualism as against the holism that informs the logic of the caste system.

Dumont advices the analysts of caste to be sensitive to two structural principles i.e., one is '*caste is tuned towards the whole*' and the other is '*ideology or value of caste system defined by the principles of ritual hierarchy which encompasses domain of empirical facts*'. This approach not only synthesizes the puzzling diversity of caste and its working but also helps to get as holistic hold on it.

French scholar, *Celestin Bonegie*, insisted the caste system "as a product of unique configuration of three relational properties of the caste separation, hierarchy and interdependence". (*Appadurai*1988: 42)

Caste is a consensual and coherent principle of thought and practice. Most anthropological work on caste *Gellner* displays a '*rural bias*' (1992:2). "Indian Village" is making both a sociological as well as methodological unit of reality i.e., a most favorable locale to study caste. "Caste system" along with the "Indian village" is understood to be the two "*fundamental*" aspects of the social reality in India.

Usually anthropologists choose a village – albeit of the some careful considerations study it, as it constitutes a self-contained and self-reliant moral universe of meaning – making and practices. If some anthropologists were to study in non-rural contexts, there was a compulsion to explain such choice. Thus most of the ethnographies done on caste invariably have a rural – bias.

The classical Anthropological perspective on Caste has shared the propensities – methodological and epistemological - of the discipline as a whole. They tend to conceptualize caste as a totality, as an immutable and essential system uninfluenced by its contexts or socio-political locations.

Access to indigenous or native categories of thought is seen to be gained from the textual sources, taken to be representing – the entire population, irrespective of its varied locations.

Understanding Caste System from the perspective of Social Stratification broadly meant a normative interest in the distribution of benefits and burdens within a population, as well as explanatory interest in social inequality (*Beteille*1969b is a representative collection). *Weber* understands castes as 'status groups', i.e., as 'communities sharing some form of social estimation of honor' (*Sharma* 2002: 12). They are substantialized entities or groups that have reached a climax of closure upon themselves.

Though discussions of caste are also found in ancient literary tradition or in Indological texts they are from a different viewpoint than the contemporary social theory (*Beteille*1992: 14). It has been argued that "the relation between caste and occupation has been much misrepresented… It is doubtful that there was at any time a complete correspondence between the two. At any rate, even before independence many castes and probably most had more than half their working members in occupations other than those specifically associated with their castes"[11].

Beteille has been a very nuanced and careful analyst of caste as a system of stratification, by not dismissing the 'systematic' understanding of caste represented by *Dumont*. *Beteille* prefers to concentrate on 'material context' of caste on the grounds of stratification perspective.

Understanding caste as a form of social stratification is definition-ally informed by contextualizing impulse. It also glosses over the prisms of ideology and values, with an interest to focus on the practices and 'material interests' that caste simultaneously inhibits and also makes possible (*Beteille*1992: 123).

Some scholars from a 'Social Stratification' perspective – particularly *Bailey* (1957), *Berremen* (1971), *Mencher* (1992, 1974), *Beteille* (1971) and *Gupta* (2002) – this element of caste as an ideological barrier of its exploitative content by the beneficiaries of the system, making caste a system of inequality and exploitation.

In "Structure and Cognition" (1982), *Veena Das* argues that the very ambiguity and flexibility of caste categories make them important - both as categories of thought and tools of action.[12]

Kolenda (1997), on the other hand argued for the importance of *'Jajmani'* system as a primary indicator of caste system and its functions in village India[13].

Irravat Karve is more concerned with the culture castes, the differences between the castes. She identified that within a region there are often several *jatis* with the same traditional occupation and same general name, but differing widely in behaviour, culture, historical tradition and its physical traits[14].

A few empirical studies continue to point to caste-based inequalities in economic circumstances (*Deshpande* 2007) between OBCs and higher castes[15]. Moreover, starting from the perspective of lowest castes and tribes – the subaltern – a number of studies of the lowest castes have observed that the control of higher castes over material resources reflects clear control over *ideological resources* seems debatable and this preoccupation with ideology seems to mystify the ground inequalities (*Panini* 1997; *Mendelsohana & Vicziany* 1998; *Berman* 1974; *Omvedt 2006*)[16, 17,18,19].

The IHDS documents that caste and kin remain at the center of Indian Civic life, with nearly 95% of the female respondents reporting getting married within their own caste. This suggests that caste structure remains largely defined by social closure, while the economic opportunities are increasingly more open, creating new arenas in which castes must operate if they are to maintain their distinction. Seeing Indian caste structure through the lens of *Bourdieu's* notions of social reproduction (*Bourdieu*1984) we begin to see a variety of ways in which castes manage to shape the access of their members to social, political and cultural capital. Much has been written about the political power of various castes (*Gupta*2005) with a particular focus on the middle castes. However, the way in which upper castes manage to establish and exercise their dominance over the opportunities to their members has received little attention[20, 21].

Every society is witnessing, Women's participation in economic activities since time immemorial. As pointed out by *Sengupta* (1960), "from the primitive times when men hunted animals, down to the present day, when thousands are employed in factories, women are found to stand shoulder to shoulder with men in all the occupations"[22].

In the subsistence economy of India, women are understood to have played a very important role in both agriculture and artisanal production. Most of the activities connected with these occupations were conducted in family enterprises so that women could not only work but also attend to their traditional roles and responsibilities.

A review of the traditional economy of India would reveal important features of women's economic participation. Women played a vital role in maintaining and strengthening the tradtional economic order. This fact is upheld by the *Committee on the Status of Women* in India by Government of India.

As per the committee report "the traditional village community in India consisted of the cultivators, the artisans and those performing menial services. In each of these the women played a distinctive and accepted role in the process of earning a livelihood for the family, putting in sometimes more,sometimes less and often an equal amount of labour in both production and marketing of products of agriculture and handicrafts. Markets were mostly local or within accessible distance. By and large this pattern is still found prevalent in the traditional forms of economy"[23].

Caste System in India–Praxis

Caste as a social system in India is a form of social stratification with structured inequality which not only rates and ranks the members of society based on selected criteria but also limits their access to wealth, power, privileges and opportunities.

Understanding Caste system from the *Social Stratification* perspective deserves particular attention on the following four features:

i. Caste as status hierarchy

Caste is seen as a representation of pure status based on religious and ideological grounds, with class inequalities being epiphenomenal to caste. This disjunction between the sacred and the profane gives Indian caste system a sociological character[24, 25, 26].

ii. Caste as a system of Exclusion and Exploitation

Caste as a system of Exclusion and Exploitation focuses on Caste inequalities and their material bases which has a long history (including *Jajmani* system)[27, 28] Two aspects of caste inequalities i.e., 'inequality of opportunity' and 'inequality of outcome' are considered. Centuries of Caste based social organization left a legacy of inequality in access to land, education, occupation, productive resources along with material disadvantages. It can also be seen as socio-economic discrimination, towards highly qualified members of lower castes, resulting in inequality of outcome. Inequality of outcome in one generation may lead to inequality of opportunity in the next generation[29].

iii. Caste in Transformation

Castes acting as pressure groups, modern occupations link between caste and economic statuses etc., are studied under this feature. In Independent India, the link between the caste and occupation has weakened considerably. *Jajimani* system has all but vanished allowing market based pricing services[30]. A variety of forces like, land reforms has disrupted the link between caste and occupation[31]. Declining incomes of artisans to influx of mass produced goods led to decline of caste based occupations among potters, weavers, blacksmiths and other artisans who compelled to rely on manual labour for subsistence[32].

iv. Caste as Social Construction

Caste as Social Construction focuses, that the presumed Brahmin superiority is creation of an orientalist discourse that privileged Brahmins over Kshatriyas[33,34] and ignored the claims of ideological superiority of lower castes. By focusing on the alternate sources of legitimacy and hierarchy these studies question the notion that the Brahminical values are internalized by all subordinate castes and hierarchies accepted without questioning[35,36,37].

Structural – Functional Perspective

According to 'Structural – Functional perspective' caste system has been functional as a great unifying force holding together numerous culturally diverse groups in the wake of external threat and frequent aggressions during the long history of Indian civilization. The structural division of labour promotes efficiency and economy in the execution of traditional occupations. Every caste followed certain occupation which was handed down from one generation to the next. Caste economy promoted occupational interdependence (*Jajmani* System), i.e. a plausible explanation of caste, for *Dumount* in *Homo Heirarchicus* in terms of relations between castes.

M.N. Srinivas, S.C. Dube, McKim Marriott, D.N. Majumdar are the main proponents of this perspective.

Caste as Phenomena

Caste as phenomena can be Structural Phenomena and Cultural Phenomena.

(i) Caste as a Structural Phenomenon refers to social patterns with a matrix of relations within and among the castes, stratifying the various castes into strata based on heredity.

The Structure of caste system is an organized pattern of inter-related rights, and obligations for the members of the caste and castes as groups, in terms of statuses, roles and social norms (*Gough, Senart* 1930, *Bougie*).

Structurally Caste system manifests two tendencies simultaneously i.e., *Segmental* and *Organic*. As a Segmental reality, each caste are a sub-caste tends to articulate mutual repulsion, social distance and social inequality, but as an Organic system the caste segment are mutually interlinked by principle of reciprocity through *Jajmani* system (Yogender Singh).

(ii) Caste as cultural Phenomena is viewed as a set of values, beliefs, practices and customs leading to integrity and solidarity (Yogender Singh).

Indological Perspective

The Indological Perspective takes from the scriptures about the origin, purpose and future of the caste system. They uphold the *Varna System* origination of castes (*Manusmrithi*), jatis and castes as fissioned units within the Varna System as a result of hyper-gamy and hypo-gamy practices. For Indologists, the object of the origin of caste was the division of labour, with rigid occupational membership through heredity. The rigidity of the caste system was the result of beliefs in *Karma* and *Dharma* as motive forces for the caste dogmas. Indologists maintain that, Castes are divine, will continue to exist in future.

Social Anthropologist Perspective

The Cultural Perspectives of Social Anthropologists (Hutton, Resiely, and Kroeber) ramifies itself in three directions i.e., *Structural*, *Institutional* and *Relational*.

Sociological Perspective

The Sociological Perspective views the caste system as a phenomena of Social inequality i.e., it studies the society from the structural aspect which distributes its members in different social positions.

Radhakamal Mukherjee in "*The foundations of Indian Economics* "tried to show the relationship between traditional caste networks in indigenous business, handicrafts and banking. In country like India, large number of economic transactions takes place within the frame work of caste or tribe. The guilds and castes of India have been in a non-competitive system. The rules of economic exchange were largely derived from the norms of social or collective living.

Interdependence or non-competition between the groups has been emphasized in the norms of Indian tradition.

The economic values in India should be understood with reference to social norms; values enter into the daily life of people and compel them to act in collectively sanctioned ways[38]. So caste in traditional India was rigid, hierarchical with unequal status, economic and political power. Each caste has its own customs, traditions and rituals to regulate the behaviour of caste members. Caste gets its survival through this behaviour.

2.1 Origin of Caste System - Historical Perspective

For convenience of study of Hindu caste society *G.S. Ghurye* has categorized the history of India into four parts,

1. Vedic Period.
2. Post Vedic Period.
3. Dharma Shastras.
4. Modern Period.

All the literacy accounts of the important aspects of caste center round the four orders in society, namely: Brahmin, *Kshatriyas, Vaishyas* and *Shudras*.

2.1.1 Vedic- Period: (Ending about 600 B.C and comprising literacy date of *Vedic Samhitas*)

In the earliest work of first period three classes of society were frequently mentioned and named Brahmana, Kshatriya and Vaishya. The first two classes represented broadly the two professions of the *poet-priest* and the *warrior-chief*. The third division was apparently a group comprising all the common people.

These three classes of early portion of *Rig Veda* were later solidified into four groups; more are less compact, with three or four other groups, separately mentioned. Though these groups were very nearly exclusive units, upward or downward change of individuals was not altogether an impossibility, though it must have been an infrequent occurrence (for a particular family in two or three generations)[39]. Only the first three orders may be said to have been recognized as far as religious and ritualistic life was concerned.

These classes or orders are regularly referred to in later literature as *Varnas* so much that popularly Hindu religion has come to be defined as *Varna ashram dharma*. Yet, in *Rig Veda* the word "*Varna*" is never applied to any one of these classes.

On the relations subsisting between the four classes the *Rig-Veda* has very little to say. *Rig Vedic* literature stresses very strongly the differences between the *Arya* and the *Dasa*, was not only in their colour but also in their speech, religious practices and physical features.

The name of the fourth class, the *Shudra*, occurs only once in *Rig-Veda*. It seems the class represented domestic servants, approximating very nearly to the position of slaves. The *Shudra* is described as "the servant of another", "to be expelled at will", and "to be slain at will".

During this period the source occupation was given different names, either through individual or provisional peculiarities. The ideas of untouchability were first given literary expression in connection with *Shudras* and the *sacrifice*. There were also various inequalities in matter of religious practices between other three classes. The impression is clearly gained that only *Brahmin* and Kshatriya were two important orders of the society. The former steadily gained influence with the increasing complexity of the sacrificial ritual, while the latter produced only off and on individuals capable of keeping themselves abreast of former. The third order *Vaishya*, was spoken of as taxable group, and the fourth order *Shudra* was denied of any justice.

There were a variety of specialized occupations about which we have no means of ascertaining whether they were included in one or the other of four orders. They seem to have been hereditary rather than by regulation[40].

2.1.2 Post – Vedic Period: (Extending to about 3rd Century of Christian era) The Post-Vedic Period testifies to the rigid stratification and internal solidarity of the four Varna. Each group was recognized as distinct, almost complete in itself, for its social life. Among the laws that were valid, provided they did not contradict the sacred precepts, are those of castes. "Cultivators, Traders, Money-lenders and Artisans have authority to lay down rules for their respective classes"[41]. It may be inferred that many of the sub-divisions within each Varna and undoubtedly by now there must have existed in each Varna numerous sub-divisions had rules of their own for their internal management. The word "*Jati*" is applied by the great grammarian *Patanjali* to such ethnic groups as *Abhiras*, whom he declares to be other *Jati*, than the *Shudra*. "*Varna*" and "*Jati*" would thus appear to be interchangeable terms. It is clear that other group than the four traditional ones were not only in existence but had come to be recognized as *Jatis*[42].

The four castes were even supposed to be distinguished by their origin and particular sacraments[43]. Social interactions, eating and intermarriage seem to have been the visible marks of an individual's assimilation in his group. The rule and regulations governing social life and individual conduct differed according to the orders in society, only the four "Varna" being taken into account by the law givers. Others, like the mixed castes and outcastes are mentioned, but their status in the eye of law and morals is not clearly defined.

The idea that an impure person impacts pollution by his touch and even by his near approach to a member of first three castes finds definite expression in the law-texts of this period, generally with reference to the persons who are outcaste.

Endogamy was being sought to be rigorously prescribed and was followed to a large extent, and that the writers were at great pains to explain the origins of so many different castes, which had sprang up either by miscegenation, local segregation, occupational specialization or tribal in corporation, because the orthodox theory has only mentioned four castes.

Gautama is the one amongst the law makers who recognizes the possibility of a change of Caste, which can only come about by marriage[44].

In this period we have three types of literature.

(a) Sacred laws of Aryans (presenting an orthodox i.e., an Idealistic stand point).
(b) Epics testifying contemporary practices of the time.
(c) Buddhist Literature.

(a) Sacred Laws of Aryans

The sacred laws of the Aryans are designed to expound "*Varna Dharma*" i.e., the duties ostensibly of the four orders. The text books of the different schools may be broadly analyzed into four parts:

The first part, generally very short deals with the ashrams (i.e., four stages in individual's life) and their duties. The Second part, forming a large portion of the book, deals with "*Varna Dharma*". The two other parts deal with expiatory acts and inheritance. Though the main bulk of the law is treated under "*Varna Dharma*", yet the Shudra does not figure much in these texts. The Varna –Dharma of the 'Shudra' is such that it does not require elaborate regulation. It may justly be said that the "Shudra" was left to himself his internal affairs were concerned[45].

Among the four Varnas the old distinction of Arya and Shudra now appears predominantly as *Dvija* and *Shudra*. The first three Varnas are called "*Dvijas*" (twice born) because they have to go through initiation ceremony which is symbolic of rebirth. This privilege is denied to the Shudra who is called "*Ekajati*" (once-born)[46].

This period sees a great consolidation of the position of the Brahmins: while the degradation of Shudra comes out in marked contrast to the growing superiority of Brahmins. The three lower castes are ordered to live according to the teaching of the Brahmin, who shall declare their duties, while the king is exhorted to regulate their conduct accordingly[47].

The importance of sacrifices and ritualism had been growing and with it the prestige of the priest. The privilege of officiating at sacrificial sessions and other religious sites was exclusively preserved as a divinely appointed and hereditary function of the Brahmins. As a monopolist of ritual procedure, the Brahmin naturally became important. He also gained respect because he fulfilled a very fundamental function in the general philosophy of life.

(b) Epics

The *Mahabharata* depicts, "sacrifice sustains both the manes and gods",[21] and the Brahmin alone could ensure the proper performance of sacrifices. All these circumstances and the growing unintelligibility of the scriptural language conspired to make the Brahmin almost a God on the Earth. The pre-eminence of the Brahmin was so great that the Mahabharata declared that really speaking there was only one Varna, viz. the Brahmin and other Varnas were merely its modification[48].

The superiority of child Brahmin over an aged Kshatriya is also supported by *Apastamba*[49]. The Brahmin might follow no gainful activity, yet as long as he continued the study of Vedas, he was said to have fulfilled his purpose[50].The Brahmin was exempted from the usual taxes[51]. Both the person and property of the Brahmin were absolutely inviolate, stealing the gold of a Brahmin, killing a Brahmin were regarded as heinous sins (*Mahapataka*)[52].

Though the various privileges of the Brahmins are sanctioned by law givers, they insist from time to time that the Brahmin shall keep to the moral discipline of his class and conscientiously perform the duties laid down for him. They declare that a Brahmin who deviates from this path is equal to a Shudra and as such there can be no harm in neglecting him[53].

In post Vedic period Shudra was given the appellation of *Dasa* of Vedic period. The Veda must not be recited in his presence; no advice must be given to him, or the remnants of the offerings to the gods. Holy law must not be expounded to him, nor must he be asked to perform a penance[54] He shall use old shoes, discarded garments etc., of the members of other Varna, and eat the leavings of their food[55].

It is well known that in the story of the "*Ramayana*". Rama is represented to have killed a Shudra who was practicing austerities[56]. The Shudra was regarded to be despicable that a Brahmin, when out of sheer necessity, had to take up the Shudra's occupation was asked not to mix with them[57].

It is clear that the Shudra could not perform a sacrifice, could not listen to or recite the Vedic text, nor could he practice austerities. The Mahabharata says that the Shudra can have no absolute property, because his wealth can be appropriated by his master at will[58]. *Grihya* sutras were excluded for Shudras.

Though theoretically the position of the Shudras was very low, there were exceptional evidences to show that few of them well-to-do. Some succeeded in marring their daughters in royal families, *Sumitra*, one of the four wives of king *Dhasharatha* was a Shudra. Few of them even worked their way up to the throne; the famous *Chandra Gupta* is traditionally known to be a Shudra. The *Abhiras* who ruled over the Deccan for some time were, according to *Patanjali's* counting, a caste by themselves not included among Shudras, though they were not Kshatriyas.

The Vaishya, though traditionally classes with first two "V*arna",* is grouped on many occasions with the Shudras. Occupations ordained for these two classes are almost identical. Gain by labour is mentioned as special mode of acquisition both for Vaishya and Shudra[59].

In the *Mahabharata*, once at least a slightly material change is introduced in this theory, where it has been mentioned that, three castes were created first, and the Shudra created afterwards for serving the others. Evidently this divine origin did not prove as comforting to the lower classes as could be desired in the interest of social order. Salvation of self - had come to be the outstanding problem of philosophy of life. If the performance of religious rites, as laid down by the sacred law, could alone lead to salvation, there was no hope for the Shudra nor even perhaps for the Vaishya, because the former was emphatically forbidden to perform the religious rites and latter have progressive lost their practice. A philosophy of caste, guarantying individual salvation to all, through the performance of duties alone, had to be formulated. Such a theory as far as salvation, which has become the most absorbing human interest, was concerned.

It is clear that according to this law-giver conscientious practice of the duties proper to one's own Varna, led to a birth in a higher Varna and thus to salvation. Failure to act according to one's Varna duties meant birth in a lower caste and finally to spiritual annihilation. In Mahabharata, the upward march from one caste to another succeeding birth till a person born a Brahmin in described in detail[60].

Even in *Bhagavath Gita* the creator is said to have apportioned the duties and functions of four castes according to the inherent qualities and capacities of individuals[61]. God separated the people into four Varna not merely because they were created from different limbs of his body, nor again out of his will, but because he found them endowed with different qualities and capabilities. This philosophy of caste takes the sting of the institution, thus skillfully stereotypes it. During the later ages, this theory of caste has been rightly harped upon.

(c) Buddhist Literature

Both *Jainism* and *Buddhism* appear to be the movements started by Kshatriyas of exceptional ability preaching a new philosophy which were utilized by their immediate followers for asserting the social superiority of the Kshatriyas over the Brahmins.

In Buddhist literature there are several examples where the enumeration of the four castes is headed by the Kshatriyas, the Brahmins coming next. Many a time the Kshatriyas aggressively put forward claims for prior recognition over the Brahmins.

It can be concluded that the matter of Caste restricts the preaching and actions of Buddha had only a general liberalizing effect. He does not seem to have started with the idea of abolishing caste- distinctions, nor do his actions, as described in the *Jataka* stories demonstrate an utter indifference towards the accident of birth; much less do they reveal any conscious effort to annihilate caste. *R. Fick* has rightly observed that it is wrong to look upon Buddha as a social reformer and Buddhism as a revolt against caste[62]. *Sir Charles Eliot* has summed up his judgment in the words "though he (Buddha) denied that Brahmins were superior by birth to others he did not preach against caste".

The complete unease of Kshatriya within the *Brahmanic* fold had made this course inevitable. Measuring their strength with the Brahmins and falling in the contest, they naturally turned their attention to the masses. In their appeal to the masses to recognize them as the real leaders of society, they must have availed themselves the general opinion against the Brahmin and made an excellent use of the art of ridicule in drawing a absurd picture of the wide contract between a Brahmin's profession and his practices[63]. Use of the language, better understood than Sanskrit by the populace, immensely helped them in their cause. It is just because this must have been the probable genesis of Buddhism that the largest bulk of its early followers were Kshatriyas and other well-to-do non-Brahmins who were dissatisfied with their low position within the *Brahmanic* fold.

2.1.3 Dharma Sutra

Three of the Dharma Sutra writers (*Patanjali, Manu* and *Yajnavalkya)* have used the term *"Apapatra"*, but in such a manner as to imply that the people designated are different from Shudras and sometimes from the *Chandalas*. But always they are exhorted to be treated like dogs and outcastes[64]. The outcastes are to live by themselves as a community, teaching each other and marring amongthemselves. It seems ideas of pollution had progressed further there examples lead us to believe.

The ideal theory of caste laid down certain duties as common to all of them and some as specific to each. Out of these some were prescribed as the authorized of gaining lively hood, and were generally peculiar to each caste and ordinarily forbidden to the others. The Brahmins must subsist on teachings and officiating as priest at the sacrifices of the castes that were entitled to offer such religious worship and by accepting gifts. The Kshatriya was to live by administration and the profession of arms. Agriculture, trade and pastoral pursuits were to be exploited by the Vaishya, while the occupation prescribed for the Shudra was service to other castes[65]. The representatives of Vaishya had definitely come to be regarded as such rigid castes that, though their members followed other occupations than those customary for their classes, they remained the members of their castes[66]. The *Jatakas* mention villages each of which consisted exclusively the followers of one occupation. Thus there were smith's villages and potter's villages. Some of the crafts are spoken of as low, e.g. of the barber, who is also referred to as of inferior Caste.

Though the orthodox theory of caste is stated of only the broad categories of occupations, yet there are enough indications that in daily life further distinction based on specialization were recognized. Traders and craftsmen are mentioned in specific relation to their special merchandise and craft. *Kautilya* enjoys the localization of trades and crafts in various quarters; and in this connection he mentions, as separate groups[67]. The *Jataka literature* reveals that these specific occupations were hereditary in this period, *Brahmanic theory* of castes referred only to the larger categories. The *Jatakas* further bear testimony to the then emerging practice of naming sub-divisions of *Artisans* on the basis of differences in the methods employed in carrying on the craft. Thus the fishermen who used nets and baskets were called "*Kevathas*" in contradiction to "*Balistikas*" who were angling fishermen.

The information regarding the various classes of Shudras furnished by the grammarian *Patanjali* is very significant. There were recognized at least five varieties of Shudras. First, there were the *Shakas* and the *Yavanas* who resided outside *Aryavarta*, the home of the Aryans. Second, there were the *Chandalas* and the *Doms*, who resided within the limits of towns and villages of the Aryans but whose food-vessels could not be used by the latter even after purification. Third, there were groups like *Carpenters*, the *Washermen*, the *Blacksmiths* and the weavers whose food-vessels could be used by the *Aryans* after appropriate cleansing but who could not be permitted to attend sacrificial sessions and rituals. Fourth, by implication there were Shudras, the specific illustrative groups being not named by Patanjali, who could even attend sacrificial sessions and rituals. Fifth, there were those who lived beyond the limits of Aryan villages and towns[68].

In this period, Indian history is marked by two developments in the ideals of the *Hindu Dharma*, which had an important bearing on the theory and practice of Caste. The glorification of gifts to Brahmins, which became important absorbing feature of later Hinduism, was largely the contribution of this age. *Manu* also unequivocally opines, gifts to Brahmins, is the supreme duty of man in the *Kali* age[69]. Another noteworthy development is the schematic growth of imaginary hells as punishments for certain offenders and the progressive application of the *doctrine of rebirth*. Penances have been always ordained for specific breaches of sacred rules. If these are not performed by the offenders, then the picture torments in hell is held before the sinners, it was an effective method of seeing that penances were scrupulously performed, which naturally added to the importance of Brahmins.

According to *Manu* the *Brahmin* is the lord of this whole creation because he is produced from the purest part of the *Supreme Being*, namely the mouth. Both the gods and the manes have to receive the offerings through them. *Kshatriya* who are produced from the arms of the Supreme Being, was supposed to live by administration and a profession of arms. *Vaishya* being produced from the thighs of the Supreme Being, was supposed to live as traders and merchants. While *Shudra* being produced from lowest part of the Supreme Being i.e., feet, are supposed to live by serving other castes.

The Shudra gets socially more degraded, though ways and means are discovered for his religious emancipation, who were divided as "*Sat*" and "*Asat*" i.e., good and bad.

The Shudra Caste, the largest section of the people was the only one which was denied knowledge. If the Shudras wanted to perform the Brahmanic rites and sacraments they would invariably have to requisition the services of a Brahmin. To allow the Shudra the privilege of these sacred performances was thus to ensure a large clientele for the Brahmin. Thus the Brahmin began to make a distinction between the Shudra who behave properly according to the Brahmin's ideas and the Shudra who was insensitive enough not to come up to this standard of conduct- the "Sat" and the "Asat" Shudra. Only the former class of Shudra was allowed the privilege of the practice of rites and sacraments though without the use of *Vedic formulae*, and using ordinary formula of "*Namah*" (obeisance) instead of recital of "mantras" as Shudras were denied the Vedic knowledge. Both Manu and *Yajnavalkya* seem to recognize claims of those Shudras whose conduct is proper according to Brahmanic ideas[70].

The traditional scheme of occupations of the four castes is laid down as usual, but with some modifications, quiet in keeping with changed attitudes towards the status of some of these groups. There was some defined scheme of status of different occupations which depended not so much on their lubricative-ness as on their ceremonial purity.

Caste is hereditary, endogamous usually localized group having traditional association with an occupation, and a particular position in local hierarchy of castes. There is no single valid theory that could effectively explain the origin of caste, the oldest system of stratification. Some scholars claim that caste as a *pre-Aryan* institution, part of the *pre-historic* clan life in India and that *Aryans* found it as a convenient basis for race relations based on inferiority and superiority in their dealings with natives.

Some authors, especially in the *West* equate caste system with the original *Varna System* which classified individuals into four (4) groups:

1. Brahmins : Priests, Scholars, teachers, astrologers and custodians of learned traditions.
2. Kshatriyas : Rulers, administrators and warriors.
3. Vaishyas : Merchants, artisans, traders, farmers money lenders and cattle-keepers.
4. Shudras : workers and labourers.

Varna System was a functional division of labour based on *guna* or *aptitude*. Any individual with the aptitude of learning could be considered a Brahmin and any individual with an aptitude for governance or warfare a Kshatriya. In other words *Varna System* was a classification of individuals based on their quality or ability; it was not a classification of groups into hereditary status categories. The Varna model did not imply any gradation on the basis of ritual purity although the four Varnas were unequal in status hierarchy. Since the groups were not based on hereditary status, individuals were supposed to perform functions for which they had necessary talent. In course of time, each stratum developed its own sub cultures; Vaisyas amassed wealth and as their status improved they joined the "*trivarnic civilization*". The Shudras were reduced to permanent backwardness as a service class. Those who resisted oppression and preferred to live independent lives retired to forests and today counted among the tribes of India. The privileged castes, particularly the Brahmins, rewrote scriptures, introduced the theory of pollution and made new philosophical interpretations of sacred texts to intensify their superiority based on principles of *Karma* (action) and *Dharma* (religion) and perpetuate the serfdom of masses of untouchables and outcastes. Thus, according to many the caste system, based on birth, is a perversion of Varna which was based on *guna* or *aptitude*[71].

Risley says that people of some caste migrating to other regions, than the one where their caste people in large numbers have been living, fairly soon found it necessary to effect marital alliance among the limited number in new habitat and in course of time these emigrants became a sub-caste usually distinguished by a territorial name, leading to various sub-castes[72].

Any innovation, a novel way of that seriously antagonizes the ethical, religious and social code of caste is not likely to be tolerated by the caste, the obstinate members are thrown out of the caste and left to their own fate without having the alternate of being admitted into or absorbed by other castes. Castes are enclosed units and it is their conspiracy with clear conscience that compels the excommunicated to make them into a caste, resulting in new caste formation in India[73].

2.1.4 Caste System in Modern Period

Brahmins were at the apex of hierarchical organization of caste and the Hindu kings upheld this institution with the help of their civil power. The advent of the British has political head of the society; things took a different aspect with their own traditional form of governance. They introduced a system of *western education* the spread of which acted as an important factor concerning the root of caste system. The British brought with them to India a casteless culture and literature full of thoughts on individual liberty. The introduction of English education made many intelligent minds of the country to come in close contact and start movements to liberalize caste and practice brother-hood of man. *Swami Vivekananda*, *Raja Rammohan Roy*, *Devendranath Tagore*, *Swami Dayanand* started movement to liberalize caste system through associations like *Brhama Samaj*, *Prarthana Samaj*, *Arya Samaj* etc. These social reformers carried various movements and preaching for enlightening the people to fight against the social evils of caste system.

In 1873, Mahatma *Jyoti Rao Phule* of Poona, a man of Mali caste through an association called *Satyashodhak Samaj* revolted against the tyranny of caste system for ascertaining the worth of the man irrespective of caste. He demanded due representation (proportional representation) for all castes of Hindu in all local bodies, services and institutions[74]. He along with his wife *Savitri bai Phule* established schools for both girls and boys of non-Brahmin castes in 1848, apart from this he started a primary school for untouchables in 1851.

The *theosophical movement* also worked for the abolition of caste system since 1893, when *Anne Besant* became the president of the society. *Mahatma Gandhi*, father of the nation, along with the nationalistic movement made various campaigns for abolishing untouchability.

Caste as a social organization with various social inequalities and differences based on the principles of *Karma and Dharma* through which the Brahmins and the other upper castes tried to maintain their supremacy by creating an *orientalist literature* in the name of *Manu script* which helped to maintain Shudras in the lowest Varna and get all the labour work done by them, Pariahs (dalits) out of the Varna and get all menial work done by them. It was unquestionable and blindly accepted till the colonial rule.

The rebellions of 1857 accompanied by agrarian rebellions obliged the British Raj to systematically study Indian ethnicity. In the study of Ethnography, much attention was paid to caste. Max Muller wrote in April 1858 "among the causes assigned for the Sepoy-Mutiny, caste has been made the most prominent".

In the British rulc, the establishment of Courts, administering a Uniform Criminal Law led to removal of many matters from the purview of the caste councils. The Questions of assault, Adultery, rape etc., matters of civil law like marriage, divorce etc., and were taken before the British courts though guided by caste customs, Courts decisions practically set aside authority of caste.

H.H. Risley was made the Director of Ethnography for India who entered Indian Civil Service in 1873. He made first census in India in 1901 and published the same as "*The People of India"in* 1908. *Risley* observed that 'caste was the cement that held Indian society together'. *Risley* defined caste with reference to *race*: he considered caste as divisive, but his studies unintendedly turned in favour of political parties and the general politics. Thus started the effective usage of caste for divisiveness and politics both by British and present political system[75].

In spite of various legislative acts like *Widow Remarriage Act 1856*, *Caste disabilities removal Act 1850*, *Special marriage Act 1872*, and ruling out the authority of caste with regard to marriage by High court of Bombay (1876). The Bill of 1925 (opening of all public places to all classes of people)[76] enabled to remove the disabilities of the lower castes to a very small extent. In the safe guarding the British domination as a prime concern, their measures in addressing the problem of caste, have been piece meal, lacking willingness to take bold step rendering caste inoffensive.

Industrial revolution had been one of the major factors for transforming the Hindu social structure. The decay of village handicrafts and hereditary occupations, unable to compete with the machine made products was inevitable result of Industrialization. This affected the social structure in a number of ways, the old occupations having disappeared to some extent. With the incoming of modern Industrial organization and growth of

Industrial cities large number of the people congregated in the cities of mixed population away from the influence of their homes and unobserved by their caste or village people. Some basic caste features like occupational restrictions, restrictions on feeding and social intercourse, civil and religious disabilities were liberalized to an appreciable range.

After Independence, in 1950, the Constitution of India aimed to secure all its citizens *socio, economic* and *political justice, liberty of thought, expression, belief, faith* and *worship*, *equality of status* and *opportunity*. Untouchability is abolished and its practice in any form forbidden; offence punishable in accordance with law[77].

The caste consciousness has resulted in one feature that has been the marked tendency for every caste to form its own association. The functions of these associations are

(i) To further the general interest of caste and guard its social status in hierarchy.

(ii) To start funds to scholarships for the needy and deserving students.

(iii) Help the poor people of the caste.

(iv) Regulate certain customs through annual meetings.

In majority cases, caste associations are limited by bounds of area and do not extend beyond the limited area[78].

In the contemporary society, legal changes, affirmative actions, several ameliorative measures having increased the chances of social mobility for those at the bottom rung of the social ladder. However, the situation is not much better for OBCs. Poverty continues to be a vicious cycle, hampering good educational opportunities and minimizing the opportunities for wellbeing of the family.

Caste studies unintendedly turned in favor of the political parties in general politics. Effective usage of caste for divisiveness and *vote bank politics* turned them as important pressure groups. Caste as thus becomes the center of an individual's altruistic impulse and philanthropic activities. The existence of definite organizations has rallied around the caste the feelings of consciousness of kind. In the desire to help, once fellow beings, forget the principles of social justice.

From the view point of modernity caste has undergone major changes i.e., it has made some adaptive or assimilative changes but still caste has economic, political, secular and ethnicity as its mark of identity. A part from this caste is a cultural association with its own history, ethnicity, rituals, customs and modes of instructions. As long as hierarchy in the form of ethnicity and endogamy remain the fundamental factors of caste, abolishing caste cannot be realized.

Reference

1. Caste and Race in India by G.S.Ghurye (1961 : 43) , Popular Prakashan Pvt. Ltd, ISBN 978- 81-7154-205-5.
2. Weber Max. In: The Religion of India: The Sociology of Hinduism and Buddhism. Gerth HM, Gelncoe Don, Translators. Ill: Free-press; 1958.
3. Hutton, J. H. Caste, Undergraduate Review, Vol. 13, Iss. 1 [2001], Art. 4, in India: Its Nature, Function,and Origins. Oxford: Oxford UP, 1963.
4. Gerth Hans, Mills C Wright. From Max Weber: Essays in Sociology. New York: Oxford University Press; 1946.
5. Yogendra Singh, *Social Stratification and Change in India*, Manohar, New Delhi 1977, p6
6. Sharma,K.L., *Social Stratification in India: Issues and themes*, Sage Publications, New Delhi 1997p59
7. Grusky, David B., Manwai C Ku, and Szoonja Szelenyi, eds. 2008, *Social Stratification : Class, Race and Gender in Sociological Perspective,* Bowlder : Westview Press.
8. Gould, Roger V, 2002, *The Origins of Status Hierarchies : A Formal Theory and Empherical Test,* American Journal of Sociology, 107(5); 1143-1178.
9. Dumont, Louis (1966) ,*Homo Hierarchicus* : The Caste System and Its Implications, Delhi, Vikas Publications.
10. Nagla B.K., *Indian Sociological Thought,* Rawat Publications, ISBN: 81-316-0227-3
11. Beteille, Andre. 1992, *The Backward Classes in Contemporary India,* Delhi : Oxford University Press.
12. Das, Veena 1982, *Structure and Cognition : Aspects of Hindu Castes and Rituals,* Bombay: Manohar.
13. Konenda, Puline (1997), *Caste in Contemporary India : Beyond Organic Solidarity,* Jaipur, India Rawat Publications.
14. Karve, Irawati, (1953), *Kinship Organization in India, Poona,* Deccan College Monograph Series.
15. Deshpande, Ashwini,(2000),*Does Caste Still Define Disparity? A Look at Inequality in Kerala, India,*The American Economic Review90 (2):322-325.
16. Panini, M. N.,(1997),*The Political Economy of Caste. In Caste: Its Twentieth Century Avatar*, edited by M. N. Srinivas, New Delhi: Penguin Books.
17. Mendelsohn, Oliver, and Marika Vicziany, (1998),*The Untouchables: Subordination, Poverty and TheState in Modern India*. Cambridge: Cambridge University Press.
18. Berman, Jan,(1974), *Patronage and Exploitation: Changing Agrarian Relations in South Gujarat, India*, Berkelely, California: University of California Press.

19. Omvedt, Gail, (2006),*Dalit Visions: The Anti-Caste Movement and the Construction of an Indian Identity*. New Delhi: Orient Longman.
20. Bourdieu, Pierre, *Distinction: A Social Critique of the Judgment of Taste,* Translated by R. Nice. London: Routeledge. Original edition, 1979.
21. Gupta, Dipankar, (2005), *Caste and Politics: Identity Over System*, Annual Review of Anthropology 34:409-427.
22. Padmini Sengupta,1960, *Women Workers of India,* Delhi: Asia Publishing House. p. ix.
23. Ministry of Education and Social Welfare, Government of India, *Towards Equality, (Report of the Committee on the Status of Women in India),* 1974, p. 149.
24. Milner Murray., Jr . Status and Sacredness: *A General Theory of Status Relations and an Analysis of Indian Culture,* New York: Oxford University Press; 1994.
25. Dumont, Louis., *Homo Hierarchicus: The Caste System and Its Implications,* Chicago: University of Chicago Press; 1980.
26. Weber Max. In: *The Religion of India: The Sociology of Hinduism and Buddhism,* Gerth H.M., Gelncoe Don, translators. Ill: Freepress; 1958.
27. Gough Kathleen. *Rural Society in Southeast India, Cambridge Studies in Social Anthropology,* Cambridge: Cambridge University Press; 1981.
28. Mendelsohn Oliver, Vicziany Marika. *The Untouchables: Subordination, Poverty and the State in Modern India,* Cambridge: Cambridge University Press; 1998.
29. Thorat Sukhdeo, Newman Katherine., editors, *Blocked by Caste: Economic Discrimination in Modern India,* New Delhi: Oxford University Press; 2009.
30. Commander Simon,*The Jajmani System in North India: An Examination of Its Logic and Status across Two Centuries,* Modern Asian Studies. 1983;17(2): 283–311.
31. Dantwala M.L., *India's Progress in Agrarian Reforms,* Far Eastern Survey, 1950; 19(22)
32. Bayly Susan, *Caste, Society and Politics in India from the Eighteenth Century to the Modern Age*, New Cambridge History of India, Cambridge: Cambridge University Press; 1999.
33. Dirks Nicholas, *Castes of Mind: Colonialism and the Making of Modern India,* Princeton, NJ: Princeton University Press; 2001.
34. Raheja Gloria Goodwin, *India: Caste, Kingship, and Dominance Reconsidered,* Annual Review of Anthropology. 1988; 17:497–522.
35. Khare R.S., *The Untouchable's Version: Evaluating an Ideal Ascetic,* In: Gupta D, editor. Social Stratification. New Delhi: Oxford University Press; 1991.
36. Chatterjee Partha,*Caste and Subaltern Consciousness,* In: Guha R, editor. Subaltern Sutides: Writings on South Asian History and Society, Delhi: Oxford University Press; 1992.
37. Das Veena, *Structure and Cognition: Aspects of Hindu Caste and Rituals*, Bombay: Manohar; 1982.
38. Nagla B. K., *Indian Sociological Thought,* Rawat Publications.

39. Ghurye, G.S., *Caste and Race in India*, Published by Popular Prakashan, Bombay, p. 46.
40. Vedic Index ii p 257, by A A Mecdonell and A B Keith, 2 Vols, 1912, as per *Caste and Race in India* by G.S. Ghurye.
41. Gauthama, Dharmasutra (Buhler's trans. In SBE, 1879) p 234, as per *Caste and Race in India* by G. S. Ghurye.
42. Vyakarnamahabhashya I, 2, 72, as per *Caste and Race in India* by G.S. Ghurye.
43. Vasishtha, Dharmasutra , (Buhler's trans. In SBE, 1882) p. 25, as per *Caste and Race in India* by G. S. Ghurye.
44. Fick, R., *Social Organization in North-East India in Buddha's Time (*trans. By Maitra), 1920, pp. 196-7.
45. Mandalik V. N., Vyavahara Mayukha, ed. 1880, p. 432.
46. Vasishtha, Dharmasutra , (Buhler's trans. In SBE, 1882) p. 9, as per *Caste and Race in India* by G. S. Ghurye.
47. Vasishtha, Dharmasutra , (Buhler's trans. In SBE, 1882) p. 7,8,56, as per *Caste and Race in India* by G. S. Ghurye.
48. Mahabharata, Shantiparva, 50, 59, Kumbhakonam ed.
49. Apastamba, Dharmasutra , (Buhler's trans. In SBE, 1879) p. 53, as per *Caste and Race in India* by G. S. Ghurye.
50. Mahabharata, Shantiparva, 14, 59, Kumbhakonam ed.
51. Vasishtha, Dharmasutra , (Buhler's trans. In SBE, 1882) p. 8, as per *Caste and Race in India* by G. S. Ghurye.
52. Vasishtha, Dharmasutra , (Buhler's trans. In SBE, 1882) p. 5, as per *Caste and Race in India* by G. S. Ghurye.
53. Vasishtha, Dharmasutra , (Buhler's trans. In SBE, 1882) pp. 16-18, as per *Caste and Race in India*by G. S. Ghurye.
54. Vasishtha, Dharmasutra , (Buhler's trans. In SBE, 1882) p. 96, as per *Caste and Race in India* by G. S. Ghurye.
55. Gauthama, Dharmasutra , (Buhler's trans. In SBE, 1879) p. 230, as per *Caste and Race in India* by G. S. Ghurye
56. Ramayana (Nirnayasagar ed.), Uttarakhanda, vii, 4, 76.
57. Gauthama, Dharmasutra, (Buhler's trans. In SBE, 1879) p. 211, as per *Caste and Race in India* by G. S. Ghurye
58. Mahabharata, Shantiparva, 39, 59, Kumbhakonam ed.
59. Gauthama, Dharmasutra , (Buhler's trans. In SBE, 1879) p. 229, as per Caste and Race in India by G. S. Ghurye
60. Mahabharata, Anushasana parva, 4, 6, Kumbhakonam ed.
61. Bhagavadgita, iv, 13.
62. Fick, R., *Social Organization in North-East India in Buddha's Time* (trans. By Maitra), 1920, p. 32.
63. Sutta-Nipata (Fausboll's – translation), pp. 46-51.
64. Ghurye G. S., Caste and Race in India, pp 80-93, Published by Popular Prakashan, Bombay.

65. Vasishtha, Dharmasutra, p. 11; Gautama, pp 224-30; Apastamba, pp. 122-3.
66. Fick, R., *Social Organization in North-East India in Buddha's Time* (trans. By Maitra), 1920, pp. 180-1, 255, 276, 278.
67. Arthashastra, (2), by Kautilya. Ed.by R. Shama Sastri, 1919, pp. 58-9.
68. Patanjali, *Vyakaranamahabhashya*, II, 4, 10, as per *Caste and Race in India* by G.S. Ghurye.
69. Manu, *Laws of Manu*, i , 86 (Buhler's trans. in SBE, 1886).
70. Yajnavalkya, Yajnavalkyasmruti, with Mitakshara, ed., by S. S. Setlur, 1912, p. 1165.
71. Francis Abraham ,*Contemporary Sociology,* Oxford University Press.
72. G.S.Ghurye (1961 : 43), *Caste and Race in India*, Popular Prakashan Pvt. Ltd ISBN 978-81-7154-205-5.
73. Dr. Ambedkar, B.R,*Writings and Speeches*, Vol.1. part 1, Bombay: Education Department, Government of Maharashtra, 1979, pp. 3-22.Edited by Frances W. Pritchett.
74. Patil, P.S., *Phooley (marati) 1927,* pp. 25.
75. Doshi S. L., *Post Modern Perspective on Indian Society,* Rawat Publications.
76. The Bombay Chronicle, 31st March, 1924.
77. Constitution of India, Part-III, Fundamentals Rights n. 17.
78. Mathai, John., *Village Government in British India, 1915,* p. 65.

Chapter - 3

Globalization- An Introduction

The Globalization comprises a number of interrelated trends including the global reach, scale of financial and capital structures, the trans-nationalization of technologies, the intensification of Global communications and information transfer, the rise of global corporations and the increasing volume of complexity of global culture flows.

As per *Arujun Appadurai* (1990), it is hugely unsettled one witnessed complex movements of people, ideas, images, finance, technology, culture and correspondingly he indetifies five ways of flows, namely *ethnoscapes, technoscapes, financescapes, mediascapes and ideoscapes* cropping up in the ambience of cultural globalization.

Antony Giddens called Globalization as the direct consequence of modernization. He defined it as the intensification of the worldwide social relations which link the distant localities in such a way that *local happenings are shaped by events occurring many miles away and vice-versa.* This is a dialectical process because such local happenings may move in a observed direction from the very distanciation relation that shape them[1] (In his book *the Consequences of Modernity 1990).*

Giddens definition of Globalization is that, he links it with modernization. He views modernity with four basic features i.e., *capitalistic system*, *industrialization*, *nation-state*, *surveillance*. All these features are involved in the process of globalization. He adds to these features the process of time-space distanciation as a prime ingredient of globalization.

Waters (1995) developed a theoretical paradigm of Globalization, as per the argument; material exchanges localize, political exchanges internationalize, symbolic exchanges globalize. We can expect the economy and the polity to be globalized to the extent that they are collateralized.

Globalization as an economic and social process has taken pervasive form leading to an increasing similarity of production and consumption patterns and a worldwide movement of products, people, services and cultures.

Globalization is a comprehensive process, which includes both modernization and post modernization. Globalization refers to the integration of Economic, Political and Cultural system across the globe. It is a process referring not only to the growing worldwide socio-economic interdependence of countries through rising size and variety of transactions of goods and services, capital flows, widespread diffusion of technology across borders but also the interactions and interdependence of people and culture throughout the world.

Globalization may also refer to increasing connectivity, integration and interdependence in the socio-economic technological, cultural, political and ecological spheres. The very concept has many sub process which includes, enhanced economic interdependence, increased cultural influence, rapid advancement of information and communication technology and novel governance and geopolitical challenges that are increasingly binding people and culture of the world more tightly making a global village.

3.1 Theoretical Perspectives of Globalization

The Classification of 'Globalization theories' differentiates three advances of analysis,

(i) Hyperglobalists (determinists)

(ii) Transformationalists (moderates)

(iii) Skeptics

Hyperglobalists

They view globalization as legitimate and uncontrollable historical process leading to a world order based on market and supra-national institutions. The intensity and dynamics of change in the economy lead to changes in core frame work of *social action* by destroying hierarchical structures; role of nation state diminishes significantly. Multi-National Corporations (MNCs) become main carriers of economic activity at global level.

All the variety of heterogeneous cultures withdraws in-front of a unique social patterns, based on markets and institutions derived from radically liberal cultural frame work. This implies that the modern and global capitalism with liberal democracy as the political frame work represents the last world of socio-economic evolution[2].

Hyperglobalist approach has a deterministic character i.e., globalization has seen as a final stage in spontaneous and self-enforcing process of creating a global society, stopping further process of selection of types of socio-economic order. This reflection of globalization includes liberal oriented authors like *Theodore Levitt*, *Thomas Friedman*, apart from protagonists of neo-classical economic.

Transformationalists

Transformationalists have a moderate approach in terms of progressivity and outcomes of globalization when compared to hyperglobalists. They view globalization as non-linear progressive in character, representing a stream of capitalistic development subject to cycles and probabilism. Final effects of globalization on socio-economic trends are considered uncertain.

For them, the fundamental changes that globalization brings in the organization of society are growing overall integration and acceleration of socio-economic dynamics through compression of space and time. However, their approach is multidimensional taking mechanisms other than economic ones.

Antony Giddens, a sociologist of modernity, considers globalization as phenomena shaped by the forces of *modern capitalism, politics, military power and industrialism*. These forces are sources for four basic dimensions of globalization namely, *world capitalistic economy, system of national state, world military order and international division of labor*[3].

Another sociologist of modernity, *Beck* believes that unintended effects of modernity forces are *global risk* and new *global threat*, it is essential to create institutions of democracy and cosmopolitan confidence to overcome these risks. It also creates *political backlash* by those whose interests are negatively affected, making it difficult to predict in terms of direction and quantity in development of global economy[4].

Wallerstein, the founder of the Theory of "World System", believes that, Globalization as the final phase in the development of World Capitalist system that started in 1450s, and had a period of genesis, normal development and terminal crisis. By the end of the 20th century capitalistic world system reaches its geographical limit, reason for crisis will be exhaustion of accumulation possibilities within the system (Wallerstein 1998)[5]. Current period is the final stage of downward; *B-phase* of *Kondratieff cycle* that began in 1967/1975, ending of this phase began with crisis in East Asia, Russia and Brazil. According to Wallerstein the last sub-phase of cycle will end with a severe crisis in USA (Wallerstein 1999, p. 6)[6]. World system reached its asymptotes and cannot get back into equilibrium, so world system is in a state of bifurcation – there are alternative roots to new structure, each has its own path of cyclical rhythms and secular trends, which is reflected in UNO resolutions of *Cultural Economy* and *Green Economy*. For *Wallerstein,* Globalization is an uncertain process of transition of world system into an unknown socio-economic alternative.

Skepticism

Skepticism expresses both in terms of impacts of globalization and its ubiquity, in terms of sustainability of unification influences which it produces.

The theoreticians of Skepticism are critical towards ubiquity of the process of globalization, they emphasize that the level of integration and openness of today's economy is not unprecedented. International trade and capital flow were more important relative to Gross Domestic Product (GDP) in pre-1914 period than in the contemporary economy[7]. They stress on the significant role of National economies in pursuing economic liberalization and promotion of cross border activity. The creation of regional blocks as essential characteristics of world economy offers argumentation that world economy is less integrated than it was in 19th century[8].

This direction of thought process makes assessments of, non-sustainability of the current unification of the world as it raises radical resistance within the individual cultures leading to a conflict of civilizations[9].

Miletic has given three theoretical orientations for Globalization in accordance with the above contemporary theories of globalization[10] i.e.,

i. Structural
ii. Conjuctural
iii. Social-Constructivist

Structural explanations perceive globalization as a lawful process, inherent to socio-economic dynamics, resulting in the development of society, through technology and capital accumulation. It has a deterministic approach, so it is in the direction of hyperglobalist contemporary theory of globalization.

Conjuctural explanations of globalization consider consequences of unification of techno-economic tendencies with specific historical conditions and policies. This approach deals with cyclic character of globalization, hence, represents transformationalists.

Social-constructivist explanations deal with, the origin of ideas of globalization, ways in which they become part of scientific and every day discourse. By setting appropriate tendencies in world economy and their classification under concept of globalization, the process become socially and ideologically constructed.

3.2 Globalization - Opponents and Proponents

The present Globalization era consists of

(i) New markets

(ii) New tools

(iii) New actors

(iv) New rules

The United Nations Development Programme (UNDP) normally publishes *Human Development Reports* on annual basis.

The Human Development Report says, "Global markets, global technology, global ideas and global solidarity can enrich the lives of people everywhere, greatly expanding their choices. But the brighter side of globalization is not without its gloom. The same Human Development Report says : "Globalization expands the opportunities for unprecedented human advance for some but shrinks those opportunities for others and erodes human security by fragmenting societies. Driven by commercial market forces, globalization promotes economic efficiency, generate growth and yield profits, by missing the goals of equity, poverty eradication and enhanced human security.

There are proponents of Globalization who proclaim it as inevitable and irreversible process with infinite potential for development, so one should endeavor to make best of it.

There are opponents of Globalization who not only persist but also assert that the Globalization as an absolute evil driving the poor countries back to colonial days with horrible poverty. Globalization has particularly adverse impact on the poorer and weaker sections of society and on small business enterprises.

Globalization represents a mega phenomenon that is shaping today's trends. Its influence is most visible in the economic sphere i.e., intensified interdependence and competition between economies in the world. This interdependence is reflected in regard to trading of goods, services and capital. Globalization has technological base. Availability of cheap, rapid and reliable communications permits such phenomena. Technology is important for nurturing the growth of Multinational Corporations, since it is this technology which enables MNCs to exploit their intellectual property efficiently in variety of locations without losing the ability to maintain control from head office. As far as Globalization influences the distribution of income between countries is concerned, *Standard Theory* suggests that all countries will benefit. Economic analysts never support that free trade makes rich country richer and poor countries poorer. Supposing that North benefits itself at the expense of South by imposing import restrictions like non-Tariff barriers or Agricultural subsidies: *Standard Theory* also says while this does indeed impoverish the South, the public of North also suffer, hence suggest a strategic promising for eliminating such barriers to seek coalition with Northern consumers rather than engaged with North bashing[11,12].

The effects on the domestic income distribution are less clear. *Standard Theory* suggests trade will tend to hurt unskilled labour in rich countries and help it in the poor ones.

The growth process takes off when the elite in a developing countries comes to understand the opportunities of applying world class technologies within their countries, and introduces institutional arrangements that permit individual pursuit of self-interest to serve, in general the social good. This enables the country to grow at rapid rate by adopting technology, attaining the living standards of the developed countries. Globalization also brings new dangers in the form of :

- Increased vulnerability to external shocks (which has to be weighed against decreased vulnerability to internal shocks).
- Role of globalization in spreading unsavoury phenomena like drugs, sex trade, crime, terrorism, deceases etc.,

Globalization stems from technological developments rather than policy choices it would be more productive to seek to maximise the benefits it offers and minimize the risk it creates[13].

The policy advice to prosper in global economy needs certain approximations:

- To give one's citizens a relevant set of skills through education and let them get-on with the job of producing whatever is useful to world economy.
- To recognize the internal risks of full exposure to world economy (to limit their integration in world economy, limit the liberalization of short term capital flows).
- An open economy has particularly compelling need for adequate social safety net.
- Seeking international actions to reverse erosion of tax base.

3.3 Understanding of Globalization

Globalization brings forth two major concepts. One is the *Economic context* and the other is *Non-economic context*. The *non-economic context* broadly includes socio-cultural, historical and political dimension of globalization. *Economic context* of globalization seems to be stronger and louder[14].

Globalization allows fully-free economic operations across the borders of countries, without any impediments by concerned governments. There are broadly two types of such economic operations, i.e., one the flow of goods and services (insurance, communication, construction, consultancy etc.,), and flow of capital across the countries. A possible combination of these two types of activities could exemplify another type of economic operation i.e., the production of goods and services.

Free flow of goods (import/export) across borders takes place without any restraint in the form regulations and in the form quantity. The free and unrestrained flow services like Insurance, Communication, Construction, Consultancy etc., takes place without control of respective governments. Totally unhindered movement of Capital across the borders means foreign firms can bring in or take out Capital any time.

The direct beneficiaries of full freedom in private economic operations are the Trans-National corporations (TNCs) with their headquarters and main controlling establishments in developed countries. The TNCs want to expand their operation and markets throughout the world, particularly in developing countries having a large population and growth prospect.

The TNCs have immense resources at their command i.e., financial base and assets, high order of human resources and technological knowledge. These TNCs strongly influence their governments to exert pressure on other developing countries through World Trade Organization (WTO) and International Monetary Fund (IMF) for their smooth and unhindered operations in these developing nations.

3.3.1 Role of International Institutions

The process of Globalization is mainly facilitated by three International Institutions.

(i) The import and export of goods and services, control over rights on new technologies is guided by agreements in the World Trade Organization.

(ii) Flow of capital is guided by International monetary fund (IMF) and World Bank.

WTO

The WTO administers a set of agreements on goods, services and intellectual property rights. Nearly 136 countries are the members of the WTO, out of which 100 countries are developing countries. Formally, the decision making process is one country one vote. Though developing countries are four times in number to developed countries yet the working process in WTO is rather defensive for the developing countries, and not able to safe guard their interest. While developed countries are being able to direct their economic interests effectively in the organization, utilizing their political and economic power in blunting the strength in number of developing countries.

In spite of this situation, the developing countries will not come out of the WTO, because it provides them a frame work for the conduct of international trade. Otherwise they have to contract bilateral agreements with other nations for import or exports every year, which is not only cumbersome process but also exerts severe pressure every year.

IMF and World Bank

Countries are free to control the flow of capital across their border. But IMF and World Bank encourage them to loosen their control. These institutions put pressure on the developing countries to liberalize their imports and take loan from these institutions; they influence the policy prescriptions with demand which may not be in the best interest of the developing countries.

Often these institutions are helping the operations of the TNCs across the borders, more than assisting the development of developing nations. The decision making of these institutions is based on weighted votes depending on the shareholding of the members. As the developed countries have very high shares, they have an effective role in the formulation of policies and working of these institutions.

NGOs as allies

Moved by the sad plight of the people of the developing countries by the adverse effects of unrestrained globalization, the NGOs of both developing and developed countries have come out openly opposing the moves of the governments of developing countries and also the operations of the international institutions.

3.4 Main Implications of Globalization

To understand the impact and implications of free and unrestrained economic operations across the borders, two operations are considered mainly[15],

(i) Flow of goods and services
(ii) Flow of Capital

Flow of goods and Services

It needs focus on three aspects

(i) Import of goods
(ii) Export of goods
(iii) Subsidy

Import of goods

Unrestrained import means the traders can import anything from machines to food. Though consumers will have wide choice, better quality at lower prices, improvement of domestic production through imported machinery are aspects suggested by proponents of liberalization.

But the empirical evidence from the developing countries does not indicate any linkage between trade liberalization and growth. Free and unrestrained import can result in severe drain of foreign exchange reserves much of which being spent on luxury goods and non-essential goods leaving little for important items (i.e., Industrial Intermediates, Import of Technology, Capital goods etc.,), which are essential for growth development. Domestic production can derive benefits only if it can withstand the competition.

In developing countries, Industries generally weak and lack access to cheap capital, modern technology and infra-structure. They have only cheap labour. So, totally unrestrained import may lead to closure of domestic firms.

Export of Goods

In Globalization, there is no restraint on the export of goods i.e., export of industrial raw material cannot be stopped or controlled which hinders the growth of developing countries. Besides, full freedom on export of food items may result in adverse effects on availability of food for domestic consumption.

Subsidy

Another requirement of globalization is government should not provide subsidy for production and export. Further hampering the weak domestic firms of the developing countries takes place by closing all subsidized financial supports from their governments.

Import of Services

The picture is similar even in this case, there may be some benefits to the domestic economic activities by the import of services but unrestrained imports may cause severe damage to the domestic economy. In the globalized era services form an important part of production process, the imported services captured the business only in major urban, industrial, trading centers, which are profitable to only small geographical spread, leaving behind the domestic services which operate both at rural and urban areas, which leads to two adverse effects,

(i) Profit in urban areas taken away by foreign import services and sent out as foreign exchange.

(ii) Remote areas will remain without any import services, which loosens their development.

Foreign import services do not feel any social responsibility for the people of the country as the domestic services sense.

Flow of Capital

Foreign money may come and go out of country in many forms, the flow of capital can be

(i) Current Account

(ii) Capital Account

Inflow

The inflow of capital into a country on current account is through the export of goods, services, and through interests and dividends paid on the investment made by the country abroad.

The inflow of capital on capital account is through the investment from foreign countries and installments of repayments by foreign countries.

The inflow through foreign investment is mainly in three forms:

(i) Foreign Direct Investment (FDI) – is a direct investment in some projects. This can be Green field Investment or Merger and Acquisition (M&A).

(ii) Portfolio investment – investment in the share market or bond market.

(iii) Deposits in Banks and Financial institutions

Outflow

The Outflow on capital account may be through repayment of loan installment, repatriation of sales of shares, bonds and investments made by the country abroad. The outflow due to repatriation of profit, dividend and interest on foreign investment may cause heavy drain of the foreign currency over a period of time increasing steadily. The outflow which takes place suddenly in the absence of any control is most risky because it shows a *snow ball effect* on other firms which indicating low level of confidence in the domestic economy of the concerned nation.

Cultural Imperialism

The term cultural imperialism was introduced by *Herbert Schiller*, which refers to the way in which large multinational corporations, including the media, of developed countries dominated developing countries.

Globalization has brought both East and West into one compartment, leading to a *global village*. Varieties of variations could be seen in the field of culture under globalization, which may be seen as Global Culture getting embedded into local sphere leading to *micro-global*, sometimes seen as local culture mounting to global height making a macro-local and can also be seen as both local and global cultures producing a hybrid one – Glocal[16].

Globalization is creating a world which is becoming more homogeneous in nature, resulting in the spread of dominant culture (i.e., Western Culture across the globe). The Integration of the world socially, economically and culturally due to unhindered flow of ideas, values and images etc., is on acceleration. This integration is *Imperialistic* in nature and not a two way process indicating the predominance of developed over developing.

Cultural interconnectedness due to globalization and technological revolution has resulted in global cultural integration. The term *Cultural Imperialism* refers to economic, cultural and technological hegemony of the developed Nations, which not only determine the economic and social progress but also define cultural values and cultural environment throughout the globe. The world is becoming of common cultural market area where same kind of fashion, literature and music, knowledge, technical products, metropolitan mass culture are developed. Political beliefs, Western laws and Social institutions, Western ideologies, Western Sciences, Western modern concepts, Sexual symbols and Cosmetic sense, Western working methods, Leisure activities, Western foods, Western pop idols and the Western concept of human existence have become objectives, examples and norms everywhere in the world at the cost of nations indigenous culture. This resulted in many dispossessed people who have amassed a few western material possessions but no longer possess any birthplace, home or final resting-place.

Intellectual Property Rights

In the globalized era the real challenge for the artisans is not only production and marketing of new products according to the changing trends and tastes of consumers, but also to prevent effectively or deal with unfair competition or theft of their creative patterns.

The Intellectual Property (IP) system is the best available tool for maintaining and creating exclusivity of creative and innovative products of Artisans in the market place for specified maximum period of time. This system in turn can enhance the links in supply and demand networks. This

IP system provides a systematic marketing strategy for Artisans to get fair return for their creativity in market place.

The highly competitive nature of Globalization compels each country to protect cultural-based goods as substantial part of its National Cultural Heritage (NCH) in the global market. Artisan sector in developing countries plays a crucial role for achieving sustainable development and poverty reduction. It is the responsibility of the policy makers of these nations to defend the interests of artisans against unfair competition as well as to preserve the cultural identity and diversity.

World Intellectual Property Organization (WIPO) and International Trade Commission (ITC) have joined hands to bring awareness creation and capacity building with improved information dissemination to their client countries.

IP assets will be of little use to artisans if they fail to cleverly highlight their IP assets during commercializing their products in the global market. So artisans should plan to use IP assets carefully and strategically for marketing purposes. The following is a list of possible ways for the artisans to use their IP assets to market their product.

(i) Trade Marks
(ii) Collective Mark
(iii) Geographical Indication
(iv) Copy Rights
(v) Trade Secrets
(vi) Patents
(vii) Utility Models
(viii) Traditional Cultural Expressions
(ix) Licensing

3.5 Indian Scenario

Facing a severe Economic crisis in 1991, when Indian foreign currency reserves went down to one Billion dollar. India had been granted *Structural Adjustment Loan* from IMF with preconditions of structural changes in Economy. Then Finance Minister brought a new Economic Policy also known as 'Liberalization, Privatization and Globalization' (LPG) policy in 1991 as a measure to come out of the crisis[17].

The following measures were taken to liberalize and globalize the Indian Economy

(i) Devaluation: to solve the balance of payment problem, Indian currency was devaluated by 18-19%.

(ii) Disinvestment: to make LPG model smooth many of the Public Sectors were sold to the private sector.

(iii) Allowing foreign direct investment (FDI): FDI was allowed in a wide range of sectors such as Insurance (26%), Defense Industries (26%) etc.,

(iv) NRI Scheme: facilities available to foreign investor were also extended to NRIs.

The salient features of the New Economic Policy (NEP) 1991

(i) Liberalizing market both internal and external.

(ii) Privatizing public sectors and resources.

(iii) Reducing the export subsidies and import barriers to enable free trade.

Now, India has a consumer base of 1.14 billion people. It has three largest global telecom markets. The mobile subscriber base has grown from 0.3 Million in 1996 to over 250 million currently. Apart from this, India is the worlds:

- 2nd largest two-wheeler market,
- 4th largest commercial vehicle market,
- 11th largest passenger car market.
- Expected to be the 7th largest automobile market by 2016.

Consequences

In Indian context, Caste system represents a rigid form of Stratification based on hereditary status, traditional occupation, and restrictions on social relationships. Caste is a hereditary, endogamous usually localized group having traditional association with an occupation, and a particular position in the local hierarchy of castes.

India has one of the most diverse and ancient traditions of Artisan / handmade products, its handicrafts industry are an important economic and cultural asset. India's myriad craft traditions and living crafts skills are vehicles of its cultural identity passed on from generation to generation and a means of sustenance for numerous communities engaged in production.

Though, India's industrialization and participation in the modern world economy is decades old, but still millions of Indians depend on indigenous modes of production, traditional skills and techniques to make a living based on Artisan or handmade products. These artisans are the backbone of non-form rural economy, majority of artisan production remains unorganized and informal with its full market potential untapped, especially by the artisans who often struggle for sustenance.

In the present globalized and financial liberalized market, there is a rise in the handicraft sector economy; still the artisans have become increasingly dependent on middle men like petty merchant capitalists who pay the artisans in wage on piece rate basis. Another problem the village Artisan / craftsmen in our society remains concerned is that free trade, mass production from other parts of the world are out pricing the products of their hard labour.

Most of the women with no literacy have become a part of the unorganized sector, though this new market economy seem to liberalize women by making them economically independent but on the other side it resulted in a new era of exploitation of women in the market economy in various forms like less wage payment to women workers, more hours of work, unhygienic working conditions, sexual harassments in working places etc.

The lives of Indian's working women deteriorated under colonial rule. Jobs in modern sector did not offset the decline of traditional industries for either men or women, but women suffered the greatest loss, because labour was plentiful women continued to work in the unskilled, un-mechanized sector where they were poorly paid and unlikely to advance to better positions[18].

Entry into jobs associated with the regulated modern sector of the economy – factories, mines and plantations – did not bring long term positive gains. Women work in factories is always limited to the most unskilled jobs and just as benefits are being mandated, women are being replaced with machines and/or male workers.The statistical evidence points to a down trend in women's employment in the industrial sector. This is a reflection both of the decline of small-scale industries that employed women and their redundancy in larger factories. Unfortunately women never established a foot holds in the organized labour. Women easily found employment in the unregulated sector whether it was commercialized agriculture in rural areas or domestic work and prostitution in urban areas.

These were unorganized areas of work with regular hours, fixed wages and benefits. Most of women forced into these areas of employment lived with physical and sexual violence. The radical humanist, *M.N. Roy*, observed that labouring women were not emancipated by employment but rather "*beasts of burden*"[19].

So the traditional Indian women lost her dignity and became a commodity in the market economy. Women belonging to progressive society worked as volunteers in women's organizations. Leaders of women's organizations were eager to join the modern world of international agencies. They agitated for protective legislations for women working in mines and factories and offered alternative employment in the declining handicraft industries. They focused their attention on normalizing conditions for these women – teaching hygiene and nutrition, setting up crèches; working for legislation to restrict the work hour, tried to improve status of women through trade unions. Civic-minded women made efforts to force women out of employment considered normally decadent and degrading and provided shelter and training[20].

Domestic Economic developments are not determined entirely by the domestic policies and market conditions, but are influenced both by domestic and international policies and economic conditions. This constraints the policy option available to the government, which means loss of policy autonomy in decision making at National level.

Globalization had its impact on various sectors like Agriculture, Industry, Finance, Health sector etc.

The Technological & Cultural impact of globalization in India can be revealed by the following facts

- Access to television in urban population grew from 20% in 1991 to 90% in 2009. Even in the rural areas satellite television has a grown up market.
- In the cities Internet facility is everywhere .Extension of internet facilities even to rural areas.
- Global food chain /restaurants has already found a huge market in the urban areas of India.
- Lavish Multiplex movie halls, big shopping malls and high rise residential are seen in every cities.

Impact of globalization on agriculture in India

- Agriculture acquired 17% of India's GDP in 2008.
- 60% of population still depends on agriculture for their livelihood.
- Occupied 43% of India's geographical areas.
- Agriculture Scientists are applying new technologies and instruments in growing crops.

Different state governments of India are taking initiative to literate the farmers. Globalization has had many negative effects on India. Although India has had immense economic growth, not all sectors of the country have benefited. The funds that should have been directed to the agriculture sector were directed to private sector enterprises. For instance, growth in the agricultural sector dropped from 3.8% in 2007 to 2.6% in 2008. This decline in growth has greatly affected farmers because production costs are very high, while commodity costs are low. This has resulted in over 150,000 peasant suicides since 1997.

Another way globalization has affected the agricultural sector is through bio-fuel and medicinal cultivation. There is a food security crisis in India because a significant portion of the land has been designated to grow crops for bio-fuel. Crops like rice and wheat are often harvested in large quantities. However, the amount of crops that are used for bio-fuel is largely unregulated, with an inadequate amount going to the poor and needy.

Impact of globalization on education in India

- Literacy rate in India at present is 74.04% .
- Foreign Universities are collaborating with different Indian Universities.

Table-3(i) Education in India - Globalization

Year	*Literacy Rate*			*Male – Female Gap*
	Person	*Male*	*Female*	
1981	43.6	56.4	29.8	26.6
1991	52.2	64.1	39.3	24.8
2001	65.4	75.8	54.2	21.6
2010	74.04	82.4	65.46	16.94

Source: *Globalization in India: Effects and Consequences by* Subhankar Chatterjee.

India has also promoted higher education through the propagation of universities; however, funding to elementary education has declined. Sixty-three million children age 6 to 14 are out of school due the reduced education budget[21].

India's problem with Globalization

Some section of people in India, basically poor and very poor, tribal groups, they did not feel the heat of globalization at all. They remain poor & poorest as they were.

The increased gap between rich and poor fuels the potential social tensions and reactions among people. The significant erosion in ethical responsibility of business is on rise. Youth of India leaving their studies very early, and joining Call centres to earn easy money, thereby losing their social life after getting habituated with monotonous work culture. In the advent of Globalization, high growth has been anticipated, but problem of unemployment persists. The prevailing Multi Party/Coalition government rule has enabled political ideology to intervention in globalization.

In the advent of Globalization, most alarming potential danger to common people is lying in *price hike of daily usable commodities*. Though the development is progressing rapidly, still many basic problems like rural poverty, corruption and political instability remained unsolved.

Another sector, the government has neglected is public health. India has one of the lowest ratios of public to private health expenditure. The infant mortality rate for the richest 20% of the population is only 38 per 1000 live births, while the rate for the poorest 20% is 97 per 1000. In addition, the rate of epidemics among the poor is increasing; it is common for outbreaks of contagious diseases like human immunodeficiency virus/ acquired immuno- deficiency syndrome (HIV/AIDS) and malaria to occur.

Despite the notable rapid economic growth India is ranked 134 out of 187 countries in the Human Development Index[22]. India currently has great social and economic inequalities. There are marked disparities among different geographical regions, between social groups, among different income levels and between the sexes. The Indian 'middle class' is rapidly growing but over a third of the population live on less than US$1 a day, and around a third of the adult population (34.8%), including over 190 million Indian women remain illiterate[23].

Hence, the inevitable advent of globalization into the nation pervades all walks of life. The challenges and the opportunities brought about by the globalization with the technological advancement, economic liberalization and interconnectedness of cultures acts as a major threat to the indigenous artisanal production. The traditional and cultural aspects of social fabric have been under great stress throughout the nation. The indigenous production skills of the traditional artisans generated from caste based professions are under great risk.

Reference

1. Antony, Giddens, *The Consequences of Modernity* , Cambridge: Polity, 1990.

   2Fukuyama, Francis,*The End of History and the Last Man*, New York: Free Press, 1992.

3. Giddens, Anthony,*The Consequences of Modernity*, Cambridge: Polity, 1990.

   4Heileiner, Eric.,*Alternatives to Neoliberalism?*in: Stubs, Richard and Geoffrey Underhill.,Political Economy and the Changing Global Order, Oxford: Oxford University Press, 2006.

5. Wallerstein, Immanuel, *Utopistics: Or, Historical Choices of the Twenty-First Century*, New York: The New York Press, 1998
6. Wallerstein, Immanuel, *Globalization or the Age of the Trajectory of the World–System*, On line papers, 1999
7. Hirst, Paul and Thompson, Grahame, *The Limits to Economics Globalization*, in: Held, David and Anthony McGrew. *The Global Transformations Reader: An Introduction to the Globalization Debate*, Polity, 2003.
8. Held, David and Anthony McGrew,*Globalization Theory: Approaches and Controversies*, Polity, 2007.
9. Huntington, Samuel, *The Clash of Civilizations and the Remaking of World Order*, New York: Simon&Schuster, 1996.
10. Miletic, Dejan, *Economic globalization through the lens of social scientists andeconomists* Economics and Sociology, Belgrade: Institute of Social Sciences, 2007.
11. John Williamson, Globalization: The Concept, Causes, and Consequences, as Key note address as Chief Economist for the South Asia Region at the World Bank, 15th Dec., 1998.
12. Rodrik, Dani (1997), Has Globalization Gone Too Far? Washington: Institute for International Economics.
13. John Williamson, Globalization: The Concept, Causes, and Consequences, as Key note address as Chief Economist for the South Asia Region at the World Bank, 15th Dec., 1998.
14. Bhagirath Lal Das, *An Introduction to Globalization and its Impacts,* TWN Global Economic Series 3, Published by Third World Network, ISBN: 983-9747-72-X.
15. Bhagirath Lal Das, *An Introduction to Globalization and its Impacts,*Chapter-4,p. 14, TWN Global Economic Series 3, Published by Third World Network, ISBN: 983-9747-72-X.

16. Rothkopf, D, *In praise of Cultural Imperialism?,* Foreign policy 107, 38-53, 1997.
17. Ayush Yadav, *Globalization and Its impact on Indian Economy : Developments and Challenges,* www.legalservicesindia.com, ISBN: 978-81-928510-1-3.
18. GadgilD R, *Women in the Work Force in India,* Asia Publishing House, Bombay, 1965; pp 33.
19. M. N. Roy, *The Ideal of Indian Womanhood*, Fragments of Prisoner's Diary, Calcutta Renaissance Publishers Pvt., Ltd., 1957, Vol.1.p 168-71.
20. "Suppressions of Traffic in Women and Children and Bengal discussion", Stri Dharma 15, No.12 Oct., 1932, p.622.
21. Madhok, Bindu, and Selva J. Raj, *"Globalization, Higher Education, And Women in Urban India: A Development Ethics Approach",* Journal of Third World Studies 28.1 (2011): 141-154, Academic Search Premier, Web. 16 Jan., 2015.
22. UNDP: *Human Development Report 2011 Sustainability and Equity: A Better Future for All,* New York: UNDP, 2011..
23. UNDP: *Human Development Report 2010 The Real Wealth of Nations, Pathways to Human Development.* New York: UNDP; 2010.

Chapter - 4

Methodology

Caste system represents a rigid form of Stratification based on hereditary status, traditional occupation and restrictions on social relationships. The caste system served as great unifying force, it held together numerous culturally diverse groups in the wake of external threat and frequent aggression during the long history of Indian civilization. It also promoted efficiency and economy in the execution of traditional occupations in the absence of modern vocational training schools by encouraging artisans and craftsmen to excel in their professions. Caste also served as mutual aid and insurance co-operative through the institution of *Jajmani* system, which integrated the various caste groups in the locality into a well-knit community with an elaborate network of well-defined roles and social relationships.

4.1 Research Methodology

4.1.1 Statement of Problem

It is an apparent fact that, the proportion of population involved in agriculture has been declining considerably in the last few years. Consequently, one important question that needs attention at this juncture is: what is happening to the caste occupations (especially traditional artisans) that are mostly dependent on agriculture? It could be potters who make *mud-roof tiles*, *pots* and *household utensils* for the community in general; it could be blacksmiths who *make spades*, *plough shares*; and it could be weavers who make *silk saris*, *cotton saris*, *bed sheets*, *towels*, *carpets*, *school uniforms*, *curtains*, etc.

This is relevant in the sense, among the 93 per cent of the workforce that is unorganized in India, most of them either belong to agricultural sector or work as artisans. In other words, artisans are a major chunk of people who are unorganized next to those in agriculture. The dynamic nature of the society is on high-gear after India started adopting policies that further the concepts and models of globalization and liberalization.

Globalization refers to the integration of Economic, Political and Cultural systems across the globe. It is a process referring not only to the growing socio-economic interdependence of countries but also interdependence of people and interconnectedness of culture throughout the world.

There is an urgent need to enquire about livelihood of the poor and traditional artisans in the changing socio-political and economic environment. Currently, the digital divide has clearly brought about two Indias – the India of the poor and the India of the rich. The globalization policy of *'one size fits all'* and viewing everything with a market mind-set, naming it efficiency, has become a culture all over.

For artisans, who were once addressed as *native engineers*, the toughest thing today, perhaps, is remaining contemporarily relevant. Are our artisans, the tools they work with, and the capabilities they put to work keep changing to remain contemporarily relevant? The artisanal production requires the entire family involvement, where the women artisans undergo multiple tasks. It is a vital question in the context of globalization. It is in this context, the present research work has been carried to analyze the livelihood and social aspects, of artisan caste occupations in general and women artisan in particular, of the Telangana.

The present study is concerned to the two skilled, one unskilled artisan caste professions namely

(i) Pottery (mud soil) - skilled

(ii) Weaving - skilled

(iii) Blacksmith (metal) - unskilled

The various parameters like capital, technology, end product, relation to market, competition, price mechanism, profit etc., are influencing the considered caste professionals especially in the context of Globalization. Apart from this, since the entire family involves in these caste professions, change may encompass the nature of family relations, bearing, rearing, catering needs of family.

4.1.2 Objectives

In Indian context every Artisan community has a different tradition, a different need and different capacity. These artisan communities were linked to consumer communities of the locale and had domestic markets with local demand for products.

Globalization has changed the need for localized activities and demand for products has also changed. The objective of present study is to explore the changing caste professions in relation to women artisans in the specified locale especially for *Pottery, Weaving and Blacksmith* in the context of Globalization. The study intends to

(i) The Socio-Economic condition of the Artisan Caste occupations, whether Globalization has improved or deteriorated Artisans living status in general and Women Artisans in particular.

(ii) Trace the relation of Globalization with regard to accommodation / resistance towards the transformation of Artisan Caste Professions.

(iii) Explore the cultural significance, hidden scientific and eco-friendly nature of indigenous Artisanal Caste production.

4.1.3 Hypothesis

In the Artisanal Caste occupations family acts as an Economic unit, production process demands complete co-operation of the family at home based production without gender discrimination. *'Artisan' refers equal footing for male or female i.e., gender free.*

(i) Global means of communication and information greatly contribute to the choices of profession. Augmentation of Technological advancement alters the Caste professions in the Globalization era.

(ii) In Globalization, even accommodated caste professions are not being able to withstand Market economy.

(iii) Globalization hampers the Artisans and caste profession by altering the owners into workers.

4.1.4 Selection of Field

The new State of Telangana, with a geographical area of 1,14,840 sq. kilometers and having a population of 3,51,93,978 (2011 census), is the twelfth largest State in terms of both area and the size of population in the country. The State is bordered by Maharashtra and Chhattisgarh in the North, Karnataka in the West and Andhra Pradesh in the South and the East. The State is strategically located in the Deccan plateau in a semiarid region. The climate is mostly hot and dry.

The population of the State is mainly rural with 61.33% of people residing in rural areas and the remaining 38.67% of people residing in urban areas. While the growth of total population in the State has moderated to 13.58% in the decade 2001 to 2011 from 18.77% in the preceding decade, the growth of the urban population has been witnessing a significant increase. Urban population in the State grew by 38.12%in the decade 2001 to 2011 as compared with 25.13% in the preceding decade. In sharp contrast, rural population in the State grew by a modest 2.13% as per the 2011 census.

The population of the State consists predominantly of backward classes and people belonging to the lower rung of the social ladder. Of the total population of the State, scheduled castes constitute 15.44% and the scheduled tribes 9.34%. The percentage of scheduled tribes' population is higher than the national average of 8.60%. Nearly 80% of the State's population consists of backward classes including SCs, STs, minorities and other backward classes. The higher percentage of backward classes in total population lays a greater responsibility on the State Government in terms of empowering and assisting these OBCs to come up to the level of other castes.

As per the 2011 census, rural population of Telangana is 215.85 lakhs representing 61.3% of the total population. The high population concentrated in the rural areas of the State, makes their development and livelihood indispensable for the overall development of the State. The Rural Development department is implementing Programmes like *Watershed Development*, *Self Help Groups* and *Mahatma Gandhi National Rural Employment Guarantee Scheme* in the State.

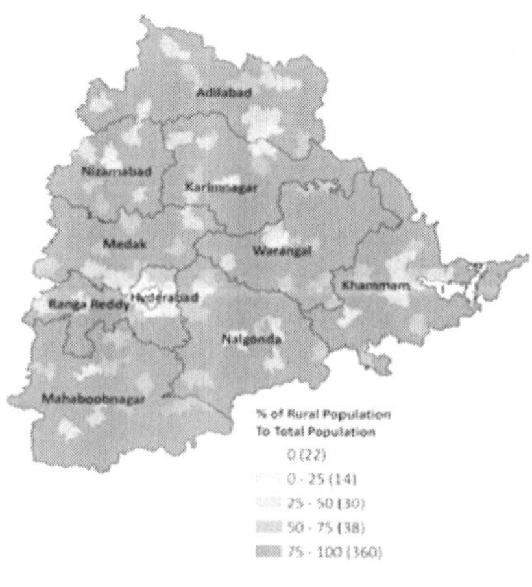

Fig.4 (i) Telangana State

Table -4 (i) Zones of Telangana State

Sl. No.	*Name of the Zone*	*Districts*
1	Northern Telangana Zone	Karimnagar, Nizamabad, Adilabad
2	Central Telangana Zone	Warangal, Khammam, Medak
3.	Southern Telangana Zone	Mahabubnagar, Nalgonda, Ranga Reddy

Source: Reinventing Telangana, the first steps, Socio-Economic Outlook, 2015, Planning Department, Govt. of Telangana.

In the present Study, research focus has been on the Artisanal caste occupations of Pottery, Weaving, and Blacksmithing which largely prevails in *rural* and *Semi-Urban* based regions of Telangana.

The Field work has been carried over

- Badanakall, Terlumaddi, Maddikunta, and Chinna Cheekodu Villages in Karimnagar District of Northern Telangana Zone.
- Kolanpaka village of Nalgonda District, and Mulamada, Rapoal, Vikarabad, Chevella, Kamareddi guda, Ainapoor, Kosgi, Amdapoor in Ranga Reddy District of Southern Telangana Zone.
- Kummarigudem of Mallikudurla village, Komaravelly, Konne, Lingampally villages in Warangal District and Pedda Gundavelli, Gambirpur Villages in Medak District of Central Telangana Zone.

4.1.5 Nature and Scope of the Study

In the view of United Nations (UN) report (1995) of the *World Commission on Culture and Development*, "the pretentiousness of the 'culture of development' has given way to a deepening of meditative engagements and dialogues with other cultural traditions…". The UN report has also made a grave and serious admission that "many development projects had failed because the importance of *Culture* had been underestimated… *Culture*, which is the soul of development, can no longer be ignored and needs to be explicitly stated in the notion of human development".

The cultural understanding of artisan caste occupations in India within the context of globalization is need of the hour. The roots of the Indian caste occupations may be traced back to the earliest times of civilization.

This country is consisting of several hundred million people, who cannot but live with and through the work of their hands. Now it's a great compensation of nature that these hundreds and millions of people have talent in their hand, but the *assembly-liners* and the *free-marketers* do not acknowledge this talent at the time of economic planning and development.

There is neglect and ignorance of how artisanal production – such as the weaving of a *sari or shawl* or making the utterly simple *pots* for drinking water – contains within itself the incredibly rich philosophy of India's civilization, its culture and its practices. Because modernity has been primarily framed as an evolution or adoption of ideas and ways of living that mimic the West, the products of the artisan being branded as 'local' and 'primitive', denoting them qualitatively inferior when compared with machine-made, mass-produced objects of uniform quality. These persistent misconceptions remain as hangovers of India's colonial experience.

Mahatma Gandhi's *Swadeshi* legacy attempted to transform these perceptions, leading free India to include handicraft within the framework of national planning. Official support schemes, often indifferently designed and reluctantly implemented, today touch only a fraction of possibly 200 million or more engaged in craft activity. In the global era, there is despair, confusion and misery among millions of artisans faced with rapidly changing markets, intense competition, decline of the natural raw materials on which they depend, and the lack of the information and adoption of skills needed to benefit from new market opportunities. With the advent of globalization, Artisans are confronted by new challenges that include those associated with technology, communication and intellectual property.

A key factor in this situation is the absence of reliable data that accurately reflects the contribution of the hand sector to national employment, production and income. Without such a foundation of knowledge and awareness, the political will is lacking that can boost investment in the sector's growth, and thus help ensure its future contribution to India's economic, cultural, social, political and environmental sustainability. There can be no excuse for the crisis in India's handicraft sector at a time when opportunities have never been so greater, and a global awakening exists of the importance of artisans and the artisanal culture to a sustainable world order[1].

Planning begins with statistical data. The UNESCO Framework for *Cultural Statistics* provides a comprehensive starting point to comprehend and lay out the contours of an exercise towards creating a reliable data-base that can reflect the true dimensions of Indian craft. The *Craft Economics and Impact Study* (CEIS) attempted to initiate preliminary methodological enquiries in this direction. National Accounting Statistics and Databases, built from the Census and the National Sample Survey Organization (NSSO) do not enumerate artisans or handicraft activity. Special studies seldom commissioned by the National Council of Applied Economic Research (NCAER) and other organizations have often been reviewed unfavorably as differing widely in their results. The Office of the Development Commissioner (Handicrafts) or DC (H) has often had to function without a reliable database.

The governance apparatus is fractured and held up in historical aberrations. Developmental policy to date has marginalized its key asset: *The Artisan.* Empowerment of the artisan can considerably yield better growth rates. Past approaches should now yield to fresh understanding inspired by current findings in economics and social sciences.

The wellspring of India's identity as a civilization, the sector has been much misinterpreted and marginalized following on *Colonization* and growth prospects modeled on the West. It has been realized that, the underlying traditional nature of artisans which when adapts to the contemporary can often pale the modern in contrast.

One essential step toward such realization is reliable data on the scale and contribution of handicrafts and artisans to the Indian economy in general, and regional economy in particular. This is needed to stimulate the fresh attitudes and investments, which can help India to enhance the contribution of hand production by considered artisans of Telangana in particular, who have created "hand producing" goods for the National market through millennia, underlying their relationship with National wellbeing.

Artisanal production is a sector that has slipped through the cracks in India's development planning over many decades. This may in part be on account of a pre-occupation with its cultural importance at the cost of a corresponding awareness of economic, social and political dimensions. The case for the handicrafts sector rests on a conviction that in spite of huge challenges the hand sector sits on the verge of an explosive growth due to a convergence of incremental inputs over the decades and new market opportunities.

The opportunity inherent in Indian handicrafts contradicts between the macro achievement and micro reality. Achievement and opportunity coexist with such phenomena as suicide rates, departure from hand manufacture, mass migration, natural resource degeneration and the absence of clear marketing and distribution system to support handicraft sector of such a scale, complexity and dispersion.

The present study is basically *descriptive and empirical* in nature. It is quite evident that, National Accounting Statistics and Databases, built from the Census and the *National Sample Survey Organization* (NSSO) do not enumerate artisans or artisanal activity. Insufficient data of artisans is available from Special Studies occasionally commissioned by the *National Council of Applied Economic Research* (NCAER) and other organizations.

Thus, the study mainly rely on the primary sources of Telangana region with due consideration of secondary sources. The study intended to fulfill the evident gap of knowledge regarding, how artisanal production contains within itself the incredibly rich heritage of the region, its culture and its role in maintaining social and economic stability of society. The study encompasses artisans: as major resource of skills for innovation and creativity, capable of lifting Global competitiveness.

The study intends to develop a unique and contextual understanding of globalization and observes its implication on the considered artisan caste occupations of Telangana. Further, social dynamics of artisanal caste occupations of Pottery, Weaver and Blacksmith, which consists of major role of women, in the advent of globalization are given due importance.

4.1.6 Research Design

The design of the study is envisaged as *descriptive and empirical* as the research demands an in depth understanding of the Social, Economic and cultural perspective of the concerned caste professions along with their living conditions and women participation in these caste occupations and also the research focus on the changing scenario of these caste professions in the era of globalization. So field study was conducted in the prescribed locale to get an in depth understanding of the artisans, the researcher adopted various data collecting methodologies for getting a holistic understanding of the concerned Artisanal Caste occupations.

The study has intended to generate the *ethnography* of cultural effects of Globalization in the locale. Given the nature of the study, a statistical sampling method was not viable. The method of sampling was *purposive sampling* since the respondents were to be practicing caste profession covering the majority of Potters, Weavers and Blacksmiths in the Locale.

In the present research, *Schedule* has been considered as the broad methodology for collecting the data along with *interview method* and *partial participant observation.* The researcher employed different tools for data collection comprising both quantitative and qualitative approaches to primary data gathering and secondary data collection.

The approach therefore has been *partially participant observation*, an attitude adopted to enquire into the world view of the subjects of this study. But then we must remind ourselves that ethnography is a practice where the risks, purposes, meanings and hopes of one's own and others are intrinsically embedded in the knowledge generated. In such cases the researcher is not always morally and politically removed from the subjects of her study. Ethnography relies a lot on the subjectivity and interpretations; the very act of writing it down is an interpretative act.

For understanding the social dynamics of the considered artisanal caste professions in the advent of globalization, the researcher has adopted *Case Study* also. Which has not only enhanced the experience of the researcher but has also increased analyzing ability of researcher. The researcher has taken one prominent Case *Study* representing each concerned Artisanal caste profession.

Primarily, the field study was conducted through *Schedule* containing important variables in relation to Caste professions that characterized globalization. The *empirical* study aimed to collect the required data from the respondents using schedule to enable the researcher to understand the social, economic, cultural importance of the considered artisanal caste occupations along with challenges faced by these artisans in the wake of globalization. Problems they face in marketing their product, their health hazards, expectations they have from the policy makers in marketing, their knowledge regarding the modern techniques of productions, modern trends they have implied to face market competitions and percentage of considered artisans still relying on traditional method of production, problems they face with modern mode of production, accessibility of women to modern production mode etc.

The purposive sampling method has been adopted based on families who maintain the caste professions actively even in the present global era.

The entire sample of this study is drawn basically from the rural areas and semi urban areas of Telangana region. The field work for this study is carried over the 18 villages pertaining to 5 districts of *Central zone, North zone and South zone* in Telangana state. These villages were selected purposively based on existence of considered caste occupations. In the preliminary investigations, it has been identified that, the pottery caste occupation mostly surviving in villages nearby Lord Shiva Temples.

Primary data was collected with the help of *Schedule*. This *Schedule* was divided into four sections, Section –A, which is common for all considered three artisanal caste occupations, containing various parameters related to the personal information like,

- *Literacy, number of children, nature of family, income* etc., are considered to know the Socio-economic aspect of the Artisans.

The Section-B, Section-C, Section-D were meant for variables related pottery, weaving and blacksmithing respectively. These Variables related to

- *Raw material* (availability, quality, quantity, resource mobilization etc.,), t*echnological* (traditional or modern, repairing, space, accessibility, power, etc.,), *marketization* (competition, trends, etc.,) are taken into account.
- Variables related to various government schemes and policies and to know the reasons for their failures.
- Variables related to cultural significance of the products, scientific significance and Eco-friendly nature of their products are taken into consideration.
- Finally the variables related to Health hazards associated with production process are also taken note of.

Hence, effort has been made to get a holistic understanding of changing artisanal caste occupation in globalized era.

Reference

1. A *study on Craft Economics and Impact Study,* Vol. 1, 2011 by Craft Council of India.

Chapter - 5

Globalization and Artisans: Impact Analysis

Field Work has been carried out to study the Socio, Economic and Cultural aspects of Potters, Weavers and Blacksmiths, who produce utilitarian based products. The Schedule contain variables pertaining to personal data like name, age, education, marital status, number of children, annual income, nature of the house etc., reflecting socio-economic aspect of the artisans. The parameters relating to the raw material like availability,quantity, quality, space requirement for storage, wastage during production, time requirement in procuring the raw material etc., which reflects constraints in global era, were made note of. The Parameters reflecting the technological aspect of production were given due weightage in the schedule, which shows the awareness of contemporary technology among the artisans. The schedule also covers the market constraints, impact of globalization and the expectations of Artisans from the Government.

The field work has been carried over *fifty*respondent families of Potters, fifty families of Weavers and *forty* families of Black-smiths. These *One hundred and forty* respondent families are scattered in Central Telangana, Northern Telangana and Southern Telangana, which enable the researcher to have a comprehensive understanding over the changes that occur in these caste profession and difficulties that these artisans face in the advent of globalization at the grass-root levels.

5.1 Pottery

5.1.1 Contemporary Status

With the advent of industrialization in 19th century, slowly changes started taking place in technology. Technology that comes from time to time has introduced a whole range of vessels and household utensils that were supplied by potters in traditional India. The pottery is gradually being marginalized from the mainframe utility items at the household level even in many villages.

The situation became worst when the *mud roof tiles* were replaced by concrete roofing, which reduced total demand for *mud roof tiles* and much of the livelihood of these communities became miserable. The excessive usage of plastic gave a death blow to the community livelihood. Consequently, it is self-evident that, potters being marginalizedi.e., a section of skilled artisanal population being left without their livelihood opportunities.

Apart from this, in the wake of modernity and globalization, the plastic vases and cement vases are replacing mud vases in gardens; even these vases are given red colour to give look of mud vases, giving a tough competition to mud vases. It is evident from market trend for past two to three years that electric lamps in small plastic pans looking like Diyas being replaced to original Clay Diyas.

But still we find potters continuing their caste occupation for the sustenance of certain cultural traits in the society and provide the required earthens when asked for

(i) During marriages or new house ceremonies

(ii) During cultural fests like *Bonalu, Deepawali* etc.,

(iii) To perform last ritual of life i.e. death ritual

With improved awareness level on the importance of education, children from potters' families are sent to schools. Many boys and girls before and after school hours try their hands in making pottery articles help theirparents increase the quantity produced, thereby learning the livelihood skill andthey are handing down the skill and artfrom generation to generation. So, the inherent dynamic skill of traditional production that operates in potters' families in the process of carrying out their work for earning a living, is being carried on to generations.

Potters usually locate themselves away from the main village considering factors like availability of water and spacious place to air-dry their articles, for keeping the main community away from the kiln smoke. Marketing of pottery articles to long distance for sales is done by men, taking articles to weekly markets at the villages nearby is usuallydone by the women.

From technology concern the only tool that the potters identified with is '*a potter's wheel* ', called as "*Sara*". Indian government agencies like Khadi and Village Industries Commission (KVIC) along with international agencies United Nations Development Programme (UNDP) have extended support and helped introduce a whole range of improved tools, machines and technology in pottery which includes Buck Machine, Ball Mill, Power-run-potter's wheel, Jigger Machine, Gas Chula and so on. These are of course acquired by organized potters only.

As pottery, in Telangana region is rural-based artisanal caste occupation, which is basically unorganized, and most of the potters are less educated they are unaware of these improved tools and do not get such support, but they have no regret for non-availability of these improved tools. They look forward from the government to have loan for construction of work-shed or shed for the kilnwhere they bake the pottery articles in order to protect the articles from sudden rain, and a bearing *sara*(potter's wheel which runs on ball bearing not on power).

The reasons for Telangana potters not so curious about the modern machinery could be

(i) Machineries not user friendly

(ii) Maintenance of which unknown to potters (they cannot repair defects)

(iii) Machines remain unused for long time for non-availability of repairing Parts/mechanic may get rusted.

(iv) Extra financial burden to purchase new machineries which may be costly comparatively to traditional one.

(v) More space requirement for keeping these machineries.

(vi) New machineries lead to more production, thereby pressurizing potter to market. As the market is already reduced, this may lead to stock accumulation. This once again requires space to keep the stock protected, as the articles are delicate.

Except in few places where still local cultures remain undisturbed like in Kerala and Kanyakumari, change in the mindset of the people has resulted in poor off-take of pottery articles and poor income to the potters.

The potters are aware of the fact that the market and modernity are marginalizing the pottery tradition and the demand for ethnic items. The increasing role of fashion trends and market dynamics keep silently communicating to the potters that they should turn to doing red pottery articles and terracotta items only for the antique shops in five star hotels, and not for anyutilitarian value as it used to be with women in traditional kitchens.

This artisanal community production has prominent sustenance near the *Shiva Temples* due to cultural form of *Bonalu* in *Earthen Pots*in the regions of Telangana i.e., *Raja Rajeshwari Temple*, Vemulawada of Karimnagar district, *Rekula Kunta Mallana Temple,* near Terlumadi village, Mustabad Mandal of Karimnagar district, *Mallikarjuna swamy Temple*, near Kummargudem of Mallikudurla village, Dharmasagar Mandal of Warangal district,*Kommuravelli Mallanna Temple*, near Kommuravelli village, Cheryala Mandal, of Warangal district.

5.1.2 Production process

The tools used by the pottery artisans are *golem, jalleda, sara / ball bearing sara / power sara, stone, salpa, Para, thatta, gadda para, and Bhatti.* The central part of production is *sara*, which is made up of donkey dung (*gadidha ladhi*), light weight in nature. All most all the tools are handed down to generations through traditional way. The various phases of production are

(i) Initially identifying the *mud clay* (kummari matti) useful for making pottery. This sight is usually within 20 km vicinity from potters' habitat. The expenditure incurred to dump the considered *mud clay* to potters disposal is in between Rs. 2500/- to Rs. 3000/ - per tractor load.

(ii) Beating the clay (matti kottadam) into fine particles, to get smooth and uniform particle size of the clay.

(iii) Now, fine segregation of clay by means of*jalleda.* (*jallinchadam*), which makes the clay smooth and soft.

(iv) Soaking the clay in water (*nanpettadam*).

(v) Constructing a small banking for segregated soaked mud clay from water, and adding ash (ash of kiln after baking, which is very fine fly ash type) to make soaked *mud clay* soft. (*madikattadam+ boodida kalpadam*)

(vi) Making heap of soaked soft clay i.e., Mudda cheyadam (kuppa veyadam), now the clay is ready for molding. It will be kept at corner of room in protected manner.

(vii) Now, this prepared mud clay dough is placed on *sara*, the semisolid mud clay dough will be shaped into different types of utensils with bare hands of potter while rotating the *sara* with stick. The extraordinary skill of potter can be visible at the time of shaping mud clay into different utensils.

(viii) After getting utensils of desired shape from *sara*, they keep it aside for air drying in shade after few hours they finely shape it by using *stone and salpa*. During this process they use fly ash of kiln to bridge the big pores on the surface of raw utensils. The traditional skill is apparent during this process which is known as *sarvadam*.

(ix) The next process is drying the utensils in shade and morning sunlight in rotation manner.

(x) Now, the final process of baking the shade dried utensils in kiln. In each baking turn, they bake around 300 utensils as upper limit. This process is most important. Firstly they place all utensils in symmetry fashion within kiln with burning fuel as dry wood and *poraka*. During this process if rain comes, the entire work goes into vain. Baking in kiln is done for 4 hours to 6 hours and left till next morning.

5.1.3 Role of Women

In the family based production the role of the women is indispensible. The women role is extremely important in following phases of production,

1. Beating the clay
2. Soaking the clay
3. Fine segregation of the clay
4. Constructing a small banking for soaked clay and adding ash of the kiln to make clay hard and soft.
5. Drying the utensils in shadow.
6. Watching the kiln to maintain temperature for 4 hours for baking.
7. Most importantly, local marketing.

Women play an important role, without their support it is not possible to carry the production. In these family based home productions every member of the family right from children of 6 years age to the aged family members who can walk contribute in production according to their capability.

5.1.4 Cultural Significance

The potters' community maintains its cultural significance to the society in general and during the following occasions in particular.

(i) during birth (presently practice extinguished)
(ii) during marriages
(iii) Gruhapraveshams
(iv) Cultural fests like *Bonalu*
(v) Death ceremony including carrying ash to sacred rivers

5.1.5 Environment Friendly

They are biodegradable, does not pollute the environment through wastages in production, the entire process of making the pottery is eco-friendly.

Benefits of Earthen cook-ware

(i) The nutrient value of food cooked in earthen ware is rich, tastier, keeps the food hot for longer time and preserves the food for longer time without being putrefied.
(ii) The food items like *tamarind, items rich in vitamin-C,* when cooked in steel /Aluminum vessels will undergo chemical reaction, whereas the same items cooked in the *earthen vessels* will not undergo such reactions.
(iii) If food cooked in *earthen vessels* gets over fried, the burnt flavor will not percolate to entire dish.
(iv) Oil consumption for cooking in pottery vessels after 2/3 times usage will be very less.
(v) Pottery utensils will be excellent for storing pickles and also increase the flavor.
(vi) The food cooked in *earthen vessels* remains hot for long time.

Since they are delicate, need to be handled carefully and can be cleaned easily.

5.1.6 Socio-Economic conditions

The socio-economic conditions of fifty pottery respondent families of Telangana region have been assessed through Schedule method and tabulated into six tables.

Table – 5(i) Age wise classification of respondents of Pottery

Age group	*Frequency*	*Percentage*
25 – 30yr	03	6%
31 - 45yr	13	26%
46 – 60yr	18	36%
61 and above	16	32%

It is quite evident from *Table-5(i)*, that there are 62% of potter respondents hailing from the age group of 31-60yrs. It could be noted, 32% of these potter respondents are aged above 61years, which clearly indicates that the old generations are very much attached and continuing their caste profession. Only 6% of potter respondents are in the age group of 25-30yrs, indicating that the younger generation of potter caste are not showing much interest in performing the traditional caste occupation, in the global era due to various constraints.

Table - 5(ii) Educational Status of Respondents of Pottery

Educational qualification	*Frequency*	*Percentage*
Illiterate	27	54%
Up to 5th class	10	20%
6th to 10th class	10	20%
Inter	3	6%
UG / PG	Nil	0%

The *Table-5(ii)* shows educational qualifications of potter respondents, it is clearly evident that 54% of total respondents are illiterates, 20% of these respondents studied below or up to 5th class who can hardly sign but may not read / write, and 20% studied between 6th class to 10th class who may be able to read but cannot represent themselves. Only 6% of them studied Intermediate education. There are no potter respondents who complete UG/PG.

This low literacy rate acts as major hurdle for these artisans to access / avail the government schemes/policies and can hardly think of global market and their approach to it. They totally rely on their caste occupation for their sustenance and livelihood. It is noteworthy that most of the children of respondents are pursing UG/PG courses.

Table –5(iii) Income-wise Distribution of Potter Respondents

Income per Annum	*Frequency*	*Percentage*
Rs. Up to 15,000/-	18	36%
Rs. 15,001 – 25,000/-	23	46%
Rs. 25,001 – 40,000/-	09	18%
Rs. Above 40,000/-	Nil	0%

The *Table-5(iii)*clearly shows the Annual income pattern of Potters. Out of total respondent families of Potter caste profession, 46% of potters having their annual income in the range of Rs. 15,001/- – Rs. 25,000/-. There are 18% of total respondents having their annual income in the range of Rs.25,001/- to Rs. 40,000/. These 18% respondents are those potters who are attached to various *Shaivate Temples.*

The empirical study has revealed that these potters can work only six months in a year i.e., from January to June. The environment is not conducive to work from July to Dec., due to wet conditions of weather in Rainy and winter seasons. The Potter Caste profession is surviving very little extent because of prevailing Cultural practices of the society in the global era, the survival of this caste profession is comparatively louder nearby Shiva temples.

The '*Iiloni Mallanna*' temple near Warangal, '*Komuraveely Mallanna'* temple near Cheryala, '*Mallikudurla Mallikarjuna Swamy'* temple near Dharmasagar, '*Rekula kunta Mallanna'* near Siddepet, '*Vemulawada Rajarajeshwari'* temple in Karimnagar are prominent *Shaivet Temples* of Telangana region, the cultural practice of offering *Bonalu,* prepared in Earthen pots at these temples enable reasonably good market for Potters. But, these days the devotees are offering *Bonalu* in metallic vessels which cause a serious threat to the survival of potter caste occupation and also serious aberration in the cultural practice as per Hindu mythology.

Though the Government of Telangana announced the *Bonalu* festival as the State festival but has not made it mandatory to offer *Bonalu* in Earthen pots only. If government plunged into action, through its various agencies, just like in Godavari *Pushkaralu,* with regard to *Bonala festival* the entire Pottery Caste profession survives reasonably. Even the Endowment Department is not recognizing potter's due rights and share on par with *Oggu* priests at *Shaivet temples*. There are 18% potters respondents who are nearby these *Shaivet temples* come under present study.

It is clearly evident from the data of respondents that 36% of respondents are earning an annual income below Rs. 15,000/- from their caste occupations, which clearly reflects the marginalization of these artisanal products in the wake of globalization, pushing these traditional artisans to adverse poverty.

These artisans continue the caste profession even in odd times and are responsible for the survival of the caste profession under Cultural Economy. Due to low marketable opportunities in global era, they engage in other part-timeworks to supplement their income.

Table–5(iv) : Potter Respondents Engaged part-timely on other works

Nature ofpart-time job	*Frequency*	*Percentage*
i. Agriculture labour	22	44%
ii. Rojgar yojana works	10	20%
iii. Auto / Bus drivers	12	24%
iv. No scope to do any other work	06	12%

*Table -5(iv)*shows that 64% (44% and 20%) of respondents are engaged in Agricultural labour works and *Rojagar Youjana* works respectively. There are 24% of respondents are indulged in part-time work as Auto/Private Bus drivers to supplement their income. The women in the family actively participate in caste profession along the *beedi rolling* work. It is evident that there exist 12% of respondents with no scope to do any other work due to their age factor but practice the caste profession as self-esteem.

Table -5(v) Nature of the Houses of Respondents of Pottery

	Nature of house	*Frequency*	*Percentage*
i.	Thatched/Asbestas sheet roof	nil	0%
ii.	Mud tiles roof with mud walls	47	94%
iii.	Bangalore tiles roof	02	4%
iv.	RCC slab roof	01	2%

As per *Table-5(v)* , 94% potter respondents possess houses with "Mud tile" roof and mud wall, only 4% respondents had "Bangalore tile" roof houses and 2% possess "Cement Concrete" roofs. There was no respondent living in "thatched roof" houses. Notably, all their houses are handed down by their ancestors. The rural artisans income in this global era is hand to mouth, miserable living conditions are prevailing among the traditional artisans of pottery who are not only maintaining and perpetuating the artisanal skill of production along with cultural heritage but are also sustaining the cultural significance of the society.

Table -5(vi) : Adoption of Technology by Respondents of Pottery

Adoption of Technology	*Frequency*	*Percentage*
Traditional	48	96%
Partially (ball bearing Sara)	2	4%
Electronically control Sara	Nil	0%

*Table-5(vi)*shows their inability to adopt modern technology. In recent times, previous governments supplied ball bearing saras to few potters, now, 4% of respondents possess ball bearing sara. Majority 96% respondents rely on Traditional method of production, due to financial incapacity, unable to mobilize the resources and non-availability of ball bearing Sara in the nearby market. There was no potter possessing electronically *control Sara.*

The low socio-economic status of the traditional pottery artisans was reflected in the empirical study, demanding an exigency of policy makers' attention for upholding and protecting these traditional cultural expressions of the artisans in the global era.

The potters of Telangana use *Mud clay (Kummari Matti)* as the raw material for making the earthen items. Procuring Mud clay is not difficult for them; usually it will be available within a range of 20 Km from their residences. They spend in between Rs. 2,500/- to Rs. 3,000/- for getting tractor Mud clay. They usually get it dumped beside their residences. If it rains heavily, some portion of this mud clay get flushed away.

These potters have a common *Kiln* for 5 to 6 families. The potter's wheel i.e., *Sara* and tools related to the traditional caste occupation are handed down to the generations. Potter's wheel will not be available in the market for purchasing, so if a person has two sons and both of them wants to continue the caste occupation, then the elder son will be getting the *Sara* and has to pay half of its amount (nearly Rs. 1,000/-) to his younger brother. The younger one after adding the remaining amount will get a *Sara* from one of the potters who is not in need of it.

Usually potters after making 300 items of various types, get them baked in the *Kiln.* Arranging these items in the *Kiln* for baking is done by men with assistance of women, to lit the fire and maintaining the temperature of *Kiln* is the task of women. If it rains abruptly during baking, then whole production gets into vain. Women actively participate in marketing at the local level. Potters could earn a livelihood only if they can muddy their hands with wet clay and keep steering the potter's wheel. Most of the potters get an income of nearly Rs.10,000/- per annum, hence to supplement their income for family expenditure they mostly work as agricultural labourers.

Potters continue their caste occupations basically for maintaining the cultural significance of the society. They, in all circumstances always provide their clients with pottery items when asked for.

5.1.7 Health Concerns

The persons involved in pottery occupation prone to Backache, Knee problems, Respiratory problems. They consume *tamarind soup* frequently to get rid of respiratory problems caused by fine clay dust. A person once medically operated is unfit to perform the caste occupation. Skidding of the *Sara* from the pivot causes severe injuries to legs during molding the clay.

5.2 Weaving

5.2.1 Contemporary Status

The handloom sector occupies an important place in the Indian Economy as it contributes significantly in employment generation. Its Economic importance also lies in the low capital investment and high-value addition thereby increasing contribution to sustainable employment and Economic growth of country and competing with confidence for an increased share of global market.

The handloom industry in India has a very long history, spanning over several centuries. As a traditional artisanal production, handloom has been serving the basic cloth needs of the people. Today, in India handloom production holds a prime place for three obvious reasons,

(i) It provides the largest employment among the traditional artisanal production.

(ii) Handlooms maintain one-fourth share (23%) of total textile production in country.

(iii) Textile Industry, including handlooms is a major foreign exchange earner of the country. It earns more than 35% of the total exports revenue made in our country[1].

Weaving is a traditional caste-based occupation and is usually handed down to the generations, maintaining their unique traditional and cultural identity. Every member of weaver's family possesses the skill of weaving and pre-loom work skill.

5.2.2 Production Process

Weaving is textile craft in which two different sets of yarn called *the Warp* and the *Weft* are interlaced to form a fabric. The *Warp* threads run length ways on the piece of cloth and *Weft* runs across the cloth. Cloth is woven on loom, a device that holds *Warp* in the frame while filling threads (*Weft)* are woven through them. The interlacing of *Warp and Weft* with each other is called the *Weave.*

Raw Materials

(i) Raw silk - Two sets of yarn called as *Warp and Weft.*

(ii) Cleaning agents - *Kranthi Soap, Soda, Tenopal and Hydros.*

(iii) Colours for dyeing.

Purchasing 3 kg *Weft and 1.5 kg Warp* can make eight silk saris with 0.5 kg wastage.

Processing raw yarn

(i) Raw silk is specifically treated, it is first twisted (called as silk throwing) then these threads undergo reeling and checking for uniformity and roundness.

(ii) Yarn is processed i.e., it is bleached and de-gummed by using cleaning agents. The silk is boiled in soap water for some duration.

(iii) Then, it is dried for 8 to 12 hours.

Colours

Colours play an important role in weaving, the charm and beauty of fabric depends on colour synchronization.

Pre-loom activities

(i) processing raw yarn

(ii) Designing sketch of the fabric to be prepared on a graph paper, usually the trader/master weaver gives the design. Weaver makes sketch of this design on the graph paper accordingly he plot dots marks on *Warp and Weft* for colouring.

(iii) Depending on the design, the *Warp and Weft* are independently kindled on a big frame (*Kora chuttadam)*. Then as per the design the yarn will be plotted marks and bundled with rubber shielding and coloured meticulously.

The work become more laborious if the design is changed frequently, at least two saris need to be weaved with same design and colour.

(iv) When the yarns are dried after colouring, the *Warp* threads which run length ways are set on the frame of the loom. This is called

Aassu Athakatam, it takes three days to do this work. The work is delicate in nature and demands huge patience and experience, so generally it is done by the aged women of the family.

(v) The *Weft* thread (filling thread) will be kindled on to *Pantte*, from *Pantte* it will be transformed into *Chitike,* finally it will be spinned into *Kande.*

Pre-loom activities are mostly done by women, aged persons and school dropouts if any. Handloom by nature supports only optimum size families. It can neither support a 'nuclear type of family' nor does it support a 'big joint family'. In almost all the home based handloom production each member of the family makes their contribution according to their ability.

Designing and looming are generally done by men, as the nature of work demands more physical strength and concentration. By the time weaving of one lot yarn is finished there should be another processed lot of yarn readily available for continuity of looming.

5.2.3 Physical Assets

Generally tools are handed down to the generations, there have been minor changes made in the tools (metal and design) when required. Physical assets comprise tools of both pre-loom processing and a looming.

Main tools are

(i) Loom (Moggam)

(ii) Aassu

(iii) Pantte

(iv) Charaka

(v) Chitikapose Aassu

(vi) Addu Gumme

(vii) Small cheraka

(viii) Broad cone rollers

(ix) Narrow cones

In terms of operational variation, organization and technology there are five types of looms available

1. Pit looms 2. Frame looms 3. Jacguard looms

4. Nepal looms 5. Nepal looms semi-automated (1/4 HP or½ HP)

In Telangana region, among all the above five looms Pit looms are prominently used for weaving. It requires 100 square feet of area (10ftx10ft) and most of the components of the loom made up of locally available wood. The Pit loom consisting of following parts within it,

(i) Donaga

(ii) Donaga poles

(iii) Satara

(iv) Satara poles

(v) Shade

(vi) Paaka chekkalu

(vii) Naadelu

(viii) Oosalu

(ix) Wax lump

(x) Iron panne

(xi) Taaru Pinnu

(xii) Achchu (vertical threading frame)

(xiii) Pinjara

(xiv) Giruka Pipe

(xv) Empty Rule

(xvi) Thread

(xvii) Pit for the loom, above which these are fixed.

The cost of each loom ranges from Rs. 6000/- to Rs. 15000/-.

5.2.4 Financial Assets

Finance is a problem only for the individual weavers for buying yarn and also second feed of yarn for initiating pre-loom processes, while the first lot is still on loom, they are usually indebted to traders and money lenders. However, those who work for master weavers or cooperatives get the supply of yarn.

5.2.5 Socio-Economic conditions

The data collected through field work using *Schedule Method* for fifty weaving families of Telangana region have been tabulated, reflecting the socio-economic and technological aspects of these artisans.

Table-5(vii): Age wise classification of Weaver respondents

Age group	*Frequency*	*Percentage*
25 – 30yr	04	8%
31 - 45yr	16	32%
46 – 60yr	25	50%
61 and above	05	10%

*Table-5(vii)*clearly shows that 50% of respondents are in the age group 46-60yrs and 10% are above 60yrs i.e., 60% of respondents are in caste occupations prior to globalization (1991). 32% respondents are in the age group of 31-45yrs, 8% respondents are in the age group of 25-30yrs, so there is a declining trend towards continuing caste profession in the younger generations of weaving community due to various constraints.

Table-5(viii) Educational Status of Weaver Respondents

Educational qualification	*Handlooms* / *Power loom*	*Frequency*	*Percentage*
Illiterate	4	8	16%
	4		
Up to 5th class	2	2	4%
	--		
6th to 10th class	33	37	74%
	4		
Inter	3	3	6%
	--		
UG / PG	--	nil	0%
	--		

*Table –5(viii)*shows that, 16% of the respondents have absolute illiteracy, 4% who studied up to 5th class or below can hardly sign but may not be able to read/write. 74% of the respondents studied between 6th to

10[th]class may be able to read and write but cannot represent themselves. This low literacy becomes a huge hurdle for these artisans to avail the various government schemes meant for them. The empirical study has revealed that, however these artisans are able to avail few government welfare schemes to some extent. As this artifact sector has a separate ministry at central government level, many efforts by the government seem to be taken to protect and promote these artisans. But empirical study reveals that at the gross root level the artisans are able to access only pension and scholarships to their children, they are not even aware of most of the government schemes which are ultimately slipping through the cracks in policies into the middlemen hands.

The poor educational qualification clearly reflects their poor economic conditions, but interestingly they put maximum efforts in educating their children. Most of the children of respondents are pursuing UG and PG programmes, some are pursuing for TTC and B.Ed. courses.

Out of total respondent families of weaver community, 84% respondents are *handloom* weavers and 16% respondents are *power loom* weavers. The Handloom weavers are prone to work only 6 months in a year i.e., from January to June. The environment is not conducive to work from the month of July to December, due to wet conditions of weather in *Rainy* and *winter* seasons. Whereas Power loom weavers can work throughout the year provided, they get work orders from master weaver. But they are also facing the Electric Power cut problems during the months of February to May every year.

Table-5(ix) Income-wise Distribution of Weaver Respondents

<table>
<tr><th rowspan="2">Income per Annum</th><th>Handlooms (42)</th><th rowspan="2">Frequency (50)</th><th rowspan="2">Percentage</th></tr>
<tr><th>Power looms (08)</th></tr>
<tr><td rowspan="2">Rs. Up to 15,000/-</td><td>07</td><td rowspan="2">07</td><td rowspan="2">14%</td></tr>
<tr><td>--</td></tr>
<tr><td rowspan="2">Rs.15,001 – 25,000/-</td><td>24</td><td rowspan="2">24</td><td rowspan="2">48%</td></tr>
<tr><td>--</td></tr>
<tr><td rowspan="2">Rs.25,001 – 40,000/-</td><td>11</td><td rowspan="2">13</td><td rowspan="2">26%</td></tr>
<tr><td>2</td></tr>
<tr><td rowspan="2">Rs. Above 40,000/-</td><td>--</td><td rowspan="2">06</td><td rowspan="2">12%</td></tr>
<tr><td>6</td></tr>
</table>

The *Table-5(ix) clearly* shows the Annual income pattern of Weavers. Out of total respondent families of weaver caste profession, 48% of weaver respondents (i.e., 57% handloom weavers) having their annual income in the range of Rs. 10,001 – Rs. 25,000/-, 26% of handloom weaver respondents whose annual income fall under Rs. 25,001/- to Rs. 40,000/- have trade links with traders / master weavers of silk. Not even a single handloom weaver respondent is able to earn above Rs. 40,000/-. The handloom weavers are more vulnerable to market risks and price fluctuations in procuring raw material. In Telangana region, mostly the handloom weavers indulge in production of silk saris, *pochampally*saris and cotton saris.

The weavers who are operating power looms get their orders from master weavers, who are basically contractors and capable of availing both Centre and State Government schemes/policies and these weavers get payment as piece meal process. Due to the availability of Electric power subsidy up to 50% on the total consumption, 12% of total respondents (75%of power loom weavers) having their annual income above Rs. 40,000/-. But they are also facing two important problems namely, *repairs of looms, non-payment of bills from master weaver in timely*. The weavers having power looms are to some extent free from direct market risks and price fluctuations for raw material due to master weaver presence. So, majority of the handloom weavers are shifting towards power looms. Since power looms are not easily available in the market and have repairing problems, these handloom weavers are becoming power loom workers under the master weavers. Hence, under globalization, these artisanal owners are more vulnerable to become workers for sustenance.

It is clearly evident from *Table-w3* that, 88% of respondents hailing from weaving caste profession are having their annual income below Rs. 40,000/- from their caste occupation. Hence, these weavers are engaged in other part-time works to supplement their income.

Table – 5(x) Weaver Respondents Engaged part-timely on other works

Nature of part-time job	*Frequency*	*Percentage*
i. Power loom workers	30	60%
ii. Working in Cloth shops	10	20%
iii. Agriculture labour	—	0%
iv. Any other works	10	20%

*Table–5(x)*reveals that 60% of respondents are engaged in power loom works and 20% of respondents are working at cloth merchant shops.

The women in the family supplement the income through *beedi* rolling work along with actively participating in caste profession.

Table –5(xi) : Nature of the Houses of Weaver Respondents

	Nature of house	*Frequency*	*Percentage*
i.	Thatched roof	Nil	0%
ii.	Mud tiles roof	42	84%
iii.	Bangalore tiles roof	2	4%
iv.	RCC slab roof	6	12%

As per *Table-5(xi)*, the 84% respondents of weavers are "Mud tile" roof houses, 12% possess "Cement Concrete" roofs, and only 4% respondents had "Bangalore tile" roof houses. There is no respondent living in "thatched roof" houses. The empirical study has revealed that, all their houses are come down from their ancestors.

The rural weaver artisans income in this global era is only hand to mouth, they cannot buy properties or think of constructing new houses. Miserable conditions are prevailing among the traditional artisans who are maintaining and perpetuating cultural identity and heritage of this region. In spite of their love and passion towards caste occupation, they are not interested to make their children continue the same caste profession and live in misery.

Table – 5(xii) Adoption of Technology by Weaver Respondents

Adoption of Technology	*Frequency*	*Percentage*
Traditional	40	80%
Partially (Spinning)	2	4%
Power loom (Modern)	8	16%

Table-5(xii) shows their ability to adopt modern technology. In recent times a 'spinning machine' to spin the thread onto 'Chituku' has been developed, it is costing around Rs. 20,000/-. But only 4% respondents have adopted this technology which made their traditional production method partially technological oriented. Majority 80% respondents rely on traditional method of production, due to financial incapacity and unable to mobilize the resources. 16% of weaver respondents capable of putting investment through loans, are going for power loom weaving, for them, their success dependence on maintaining relation with Master weaver and overcoming the Electric Power problems.

In rural Telangana region at the grass root level during the field survey not even single 'co-operative society' was found working, even if there were one or two 'co-operatives society' in total survey they became defunct long back and are closed.

5.2.6 Factors for the decline of Handloom

The reasons for the deteriorating conditions of handloom weavers and their shifting to power loom are

(a) With the extinction of joint family system it becomes difficult for nuclear family to meet the requirements of pre-loom activities and makes looming more drudgery along with child caring and rearing, which makes the situation more worse.

(b) Most of the 'Co-operative societies' became defunct.

(c) higher wages offered in power loom sector due to more production per loom per worker per day.

(d) less drudgery involved in power looms sector compared to handloom operations.

(f) Year after year, there is considerable encroachment of power loom in the hand loom sector. One of the worst forms of encroachment is that certain orders meant specifically for handlooms are procured by master weavers of power looms, who execute the order carried out in power looms with a tag attached to it as "Handloom product". This is prevalent not only in domestic market sales, but also in export items. The deemed exporters although are aware of it.

The present *Ethnographic* study has revealed that, most of the handloom weavers of Telangana region are weaving silk. As silk is soft and could be weaved with comparatively less physical strain when compared with cotton cloth. Cotton is coarse and hard requiring more physical strength, it requires 3 times more time and effort when compared with silk and leaving negligible margin. So weavers of Telangana in general and rural weavers in particular have given up cotton weaving and weave silk saris which makes them earn Rs.7000/- per month. They spend Rs.16,000/- to Rs.18,000/- for procuring raw yarn, dyes, soaps etc., and make 8 silk saris in a period of *1½ to 2* months by working for 10 hours a day.

They make these saris on order from textile traders / master weavers. The colors and design pattern are decided by trader / master weaver only. Weavers are paid by these traders on the basis of piece rate the trader pays

Rs. 3000/- to Rs. 4000/- per sari based on the design. The weaver has to purchase raw material himself.

There is a stringent method of finding flaws, in the woven saris (almost a sort of harassment) at the receiving end by trader / master weaver and cuts Rs.100/- per even a small thread disturbance in saris. Before paying the saris will be tested through '*Light Scanning*' for counting the flaws and amount will be deducted. The opinion of majority of weaver respondents in Telangana region, handloom weaving is a *'sector that keeps them scarcely fed, barely dressed and poorly housed for lifelong'*.

The major wholesalers and master weavers, hire the handloom weavers on a regular basis for producing the silk saris of various designs and qualities.

5.2.7 Power looms

The *empirical study* of the power looms has revealed that, Fabric like cotton, polyester are weaved on power looms, based on the item being weaved i.e., towels, bed sheets, saris and lounges different power looms are used. The size of power loom in length varies depending on items woven. These power looms have designing plates called as "jaguart". Generally, 6 power looms for weaving towels could be placed in 100 square yards space and could be managed by two workers.

Industrial cooperative societies or master weavers establish some power looms in sheds and employ weavers on piece rate system and get the orders done by them. Each loom could weave an item in an hour, the worker weaver has to check the threading / yarn continuity and correct it when required. Each power loom works for 10 to 12 hours and the employed weaver has to stand whole time and check the yarn continuity and working of machines. There may be shifts of working.

An independent weaver may also venture to establish his own power looms and may get the orders from temples etc., through a master weaver who acts as a middleman between temple authorities and weavers. Completely processed yarn along with designing plates will be provided to the weaver who has to complete the weaving order of that particular item in the stipulated period of time and the finished goods is collected by the master weaver. The power loom weaver will be provided with 50% subsidy on current bill by the government, which has to be paid by the weaver himself. He may even employ workers who are also weavers to run the looms and pay them on piece rate system. The master weaver makes the payment either weekly or on monthly basis.

Sometimes the master weaver who is acting as middleman and getting the temple orders or other orders fulfilled may help the weavers to get 50% financial assistance from the concerned party to purchase a new power loom for speeding up the orders. Master Weaver at times also helps in getting the repairing done by providing mechanics but payment is made by the weaver himself.

Power looms are not so safer as traditional looms i.e., the safety and security of power looms is less comparatively. The workers of power looms are not covered by handloom insurance.

Handloom insurance provides a risk insurance of Rs. 60,000/- to each registered (at Department of Jute, Ministry of Textiles) handloom weaver who pays an insurance of Rs. 200/- per annum.

Generally, these power loom weavers get the orders throughout the year. They will be in contact with 2 or 3 master weavers to get orders for work. Most of the power loom weavers purchase second hand power looms from Surat, Mumbai and Bewandi. The cost of which may range from Rs. 50,000/- to 1,00,000/- depending on the length of power loom.

5.2.8 Health Issues of weavers

1. The handloom weavers suffer from spine related problems due to their compulsion to sit for long hours nearly 10 hours per day for weaving on the loom without any back support.
2. Due to microscopic nature of work they suffer from sight problems after certain age, which hampers their ability to perform the caste occupation.
3. Pre-loom activities of Boiling, cleaning and dyeing may cause serious lung infections and lung related diseases due to pungent smell, smoke and chemicals of dyeing in long run.

5.3 Black smithy

5.3.1 Contemporary status

Indian farmers in traditional agriculture used a handful of tools such as plough, spade, sickle and a pair of bullocks to plough. Blacksmiths and carpenters known to be *native engineers* used to provide and repair all tools and implements required for carrying out agriculture. Farmers often used to visit blacksmiths and carpenters every morning before going for farming to get their implements repaired. There was a caste-based inter-dependency of these communities. The modernization of agriculture in the global era has changed the tools and implements. Instead of traditional bullock carts and tools, tractors and machineries are increasingly used for farming. This made the agricultural implements and tool production to slip from the traditional blacksmith artisan's hands into the hands of big factories.

The repair of tire wheels is attended to by an Automobile workshop and not by traditional blacksmiths. Tractor replaced bullock carts, thereby no bullocks required for pulling carts which made the horse-shoe nail demand die out, a product slipped from the hands of traditional blacksmiths. This situation made the blacksmiths nomadic with less work at hand; they have to migrate to different regions (urban) for livelihood. Some of them leading their life on the road sides in the tottering tents made of torn polythene sheets. They cook, eat, bath, sleep, copulate, work and even market in these tents on road sides. Most of the times, they are forced to shift their locations by the local municipal authorities. These disappearing artificers face constant threat of evacuation by the civic authorities and are shifted to areas where there is no water, no electricity, no work, nothing. They come back to footpath after a while. They make their living by repairing iron tools and implements like Sickle, Axe, Spade, Knife, and Knife sharpening for the local people. They even repair the implements of municipal people, free of cost.

Some blacksmiths in some urban areas live a settled life by residing in some areas or colonies and establishing their work-sheds near the road sides. Usually 5 to 10 families reside in one area with different work-sheds in different locations of the locale.

5.3.2 Production process

The Blacksmiths produce in work-sheds; these work-sheds are generally away from their residences. They go to the work-shed every morning with no assurance of getting any work that day in this present globalized era. If they get any work, they carry it out and divide the wages among themselves. Usually five persons work in one shed,

- One main person (who sits before the *Anvil*),
- Two helpers (some time only one helper) for hammering hot iron
- One person to blow air to keep iron hot
- One person is exclusively for collecting the coal

The person who sits for blowing air is either aged person retired from same work or women or boys between 9 to 15 years age (school dropouts). Depending on the season they may earn from around Rs. 100 to Rs.1,000/

- per day. Generally they work throughout the year, from morning 8.00 am to evening 8.00pm.

Raw materials

Raw material used by this community for production is Iron and charcoal. They purchase the Iron either form Iron shop or from *Kabadiwala*. New Iron costs around Rs.40 to 50 per Kg, whereas Old iron from *Kabadiwala* costs Rs. 30 per Kg. One third of this raw material gets **wasted** in the production process of heating and quenching.

In olden days they used to produce their own charcoal by burning teak or timber, but now they have to purchase it. Getting good quality charcoal is difficult, one person is exclusively kept for collecting coal from various sources. The cost of coal is very high. They spend on coal at least Rs.200/ - per day.

Various Phases of Production:

(i) Collecting coal
(ii) Procuring Iron
(iii) Air blowing
(iv) Burning the Iron red hot
(v) Hammering red hot iron (Gannu beating)
(vi) Shaping
(vii) Quenching

Tools used are

(i) Anvil (Daakali)
(ii) Blower
(iii) 10 tongs of different sizes
(iv) Hammers
(v) Small water quench

Organization of production– In general

- Individual home base production unit.
- Size of the workshop and the tools gamut depends on intensity of use
- Part-time specialization, full-time before sowing and harvest seasons.

- Apprenticeship process starting with operation of bellow at an age of 9 years
- Women not allowed but exceptionally in certain situations we find them work in certain sections.
- Raw material Iron either procured from local market or brought by the clients themselves.

5.3.3 Distribution Relations

- Traditional oral contract renewed symbolically every year (in rural areas)
- Manufacturing (in more cases) made according to orders.
- In some cases surplus is produced and marketed personally in the work-sheds or fair markets / roaming and selling in streets.
- Payment in grains twice a year (i.e., after each harvest) fixed in number of ploughs manufactured/repaired (earlier practice).
- Payment in cash from clients of non-agricultural social groups.
- Exclusive production and repair of items related to agriculture.

5.3.4 Role of Women

Generally women not allowed in the smithy and in exceptional situations they perform works like *collecting coal, Gannu beating, blowing air, marketing the products by carrying to the local markets, fairs or to houses in local.*

5.3.5 Socio-Economic conditions

The data collected through field work from forty blacksmith respondent families in the Telangana region using *Schedule Methodology* has been tabulated reflecting socio-economic and technological aspects of these artisans.

Table – 5(xiii) : Age wise classification of Blacksmith Respondents

Age group	*Frequency*	*Percentage*
25 – 30yr	02	5%
31 - 45yr	10	25%
46 – 60yr	21	52.5%
61and above	07	17.5%

It is quite evident from *Table-5(xiii)* that, 70% of blacksmith respondents are above 45yrs of age, which indicates that these blacksmiths are practicing the caste occupation prior to modernization of agriculture i.e., before the advent of globalization. In the last 20yrs, various changes in the agriculture sector like more commercial crop cultivation, conversion of agriculture land to *Special Economic Zone* sector / Industrial zones had adverse impact on the livelihood of blacksmiths. This fact is clearly evident through decrease in percentage of respondents from younger age groups (i.e., only 25% and 5% are in 31-45yrs, 25-30yrs respectively). This clearly indicates that the young generations are not willing to continue the profession.

Table –5(xiv) Educational Status of Blacksmith Respondents

Educational qualification	*Frequency*	*Percentage*
Illiterate	09	22.5%
Up to 5th class	10	25%
6th to 10th class	18	45%
Inter	03	7.5%
UG / PG	Nil	0%

As per *Table-5(xiv)*, the empirical study has revealed that there is 22.5% absolute illiteracy among blacksmiths respondents. 25% can hardly sign and may not be able to read/write. 45% of the respondents who studied between 6th to 10thclass may be able to read/write, only 7.5% of respondents studied up to Intermediate. Notably, most of the children of respondents are not pursing education seriously, because of the nomadic nature of the community for sustenance in Globalization.

This low literacy is a huge hindrance for these artisans to represent themselves and fight for the cause to safeguard their occupational identity and cultural heritage of their caste occupations. Hardly there are any schemes or policies of the government, both state and centre, for safeguarding these blacksmith artisans.

Table – 5(xv) Income-wise Distribution of Blacksmith Respondents

Income per Annum	*Frequency*	*Percentage*
Rs. Up to 15,000/-	16	40%
Rs.15,001 – 25,000/-	20	50%
Rs.25,001 – 40,000/-	04	10%
Rs. Above 40,000/-	0	0%

The *Table-5(xv)*clearly shows the Annual income pattern of blacksmiths. Out of total respondent families of blacksmith caste profession, 50% of blacksmith having their annual income between Rs. 15,001 – Rs. 25,000/-. There are 40% of respondents who have their annual income in the range of up to Rs.15,000/-. Only 10% of the respondents come under the annual income range of Rs.25,001/-to Rs.40,000/-.

The majority of blacksmiths are having their work from onset of agricultural activities. When agriculture was purely traditional based, they used to get workin preparing *Karllu, Dhantheypalugu, Sickels, Water rings Sanchelu, Sceptic Sanchelu etc.*

The blacksmiths are prone to work only 6 to 8 months in a year. The Blacksmithy profession is hardly surviving in the advent of modernization of Agriculture and machine made kitchenware in the globalized era. They are becoming semi-nomadic and slowly losing their cultural identity in the society. Probably, this generation may be the last generation in performing this caste occupation, due to low marketable opportunities, they engage in other works for sustenance. It is clearly evident that 40% of respondents are having annual income below Rs.15,000/-,to supplement their income some blacksmiths engage in other part-time works.

Table – 5(xvi) Blacksmiths Engaged part-timely on other works

	Nature ofpart-time occupation	*Frequency*	*Percentage*
i.	Agriculture labour	0	0%
ii.	Rojgar yojana works	0	0%
iii.	Welding shop /Carpentary	30	75%
iv.	No scope to do any other work	10	25%

*Table –5(xvi)*provides the information that, remarkably, 75% of respondents are engaging alternatingly in welding works / carpentry works. It is noticeable that 25% of respondents have no scope to do any other work due to their age factor but practice only caste profession as a self-esteem.

It was also observed during fieldwork that, the number of working blacksmiths within a village can range widely from two to three only. However, overall the number of working smithies is rapidly declining since younger generations are opting to work as rod benders in building constructions, as welders, fitters and join the companies making grills or car tinkering workshops.

Table -5(xvii) Nature of the Houses of Blacksmith Respondents

	Nature of house	*Frequency*	*Percentage*
i.	Thatched/Asbestas sheet roof	05	12.5%
ii.	Mud tiles roof with mud walls	31	77.5%
iii.	Bangalore tiles roof	03	7.5%
iv.	RCC slab roof	01	2.5%

As per *Table-5(xvii)* , 77.5% respondents of blacksmiths are possess "Mud tile" roof with mud wall houses , only 7.5% respondents had "Bangalore tile" roof houses and 2.5% possess "Cement Concrete" roofs, 12.5% respondents live in "thatched roof" houses. It is noteworthy that, all their houses are inherited ancestral properties. Their living conditions reflect the extent to which these blacksmiths artisans are marginalized in globalization.

Table-5(xviii) Adoption of Technology by Blacksmith Respondents

Adoption of Technology	*Frequency*	*Percentage*
Traditional	40	100%
Modern machines like	0	0%

Table-5(xviii) shows their inability to adopt modern technology due to financial constraints. Remarkably, 100% respondents rely on Traditional method of production, due to financial incapacity, unable to mobilize the resources and unaware of technological developments.

The empirical study has shown that the technological advancement brought about by the globalization has totally brought the blacksmith artisans to a dead-end by transforming their livelihood into the pockets of corporate companies.

5.3.6 Health Issues of Blacksmiths

As the nature of work demands huge physical strength, they get more physically strained by the end of the day and to relieve themselves from body pains they habituated to alcohol of cheap quality liquor, which results in adverse chronic diseases.

Known for their skills since 300 AD blacksmiths of Telangana had a glorious past, the trade is in danger of being wiped out completely. Extreme poverty of traditional blacksmiths due to very less work at hand is forcing these artisans to shift to other works for livelihood, which not only affects the social fabric but also leads to artifact diminishing (loss of skill). This will be a huge loss which cannot be priced. Wiping out of a traditional artisanal skill which has been developed since ages and perpetuated through civilizations will definitely have adverse impact on the society. Hence, it is the responsibility of the government to protect this indigenous traditional skill. Modern manufacturing technological advancement is rendering blacksmith skills obsolete. There is an urgent need to conserve and revive the indigenous technology of blacksmiths along with its cultural heritage.

5.4 Case Studies

Case Study- 1 (Potter)

Marapaka Mondaiah, one of the respondents of Pottery, resident of Kummarigudem of Mallikudurla village, Dharmasagar mandal in Warangal district. He learnt caste occupation helping his parents as a child and continues the same caste occupation for livelihood. Marapaka Mondaiah, who is 65 years old, is a proficient artisan capable of making earthen item based on the purpose.

He along with his wife Sarojana makes *Mud tiles, earthen cookware, Toddy pots, Water storage golems, ranjans, egg collecting trays for poultry, hukka vessels, spitting vessels, etc.,* and he is also capable of making any earthen item based on the purpose. Mondaiah spends nearly Rs. 2,500/- per tractor mud clay (*kummari matti*), which is available at nearby ponds (*cheruvukunta*).

He says that, performing the caste occupation, which is home based production, mandatorily requires women support. Women actively participate in production process on par with men as such there is no gender discrepancy in the rural home based caste occupational production. Depending on the intricacies of the work, it is distributed among the members of the family in which each and every member of the family contributes according to their capability.

He shares that since last 20 years, the market for their products is slowly decreasing. The first decline in the market for earthen products started with modern concrete roofing constructions, which eventually percolated into the rural areas resulting in the closure of requirement of mud tiles. Mud tile production used to contribute major share of income for the potters.

Mondaiah says that, Steel has snatched the kitchen cookware from their hands. Now in the global era plastic is giving them a very tough competition. He expressed his helplessness while sharing how toddy is being collected in used Pepsi and *ThumsUp* bottles by toddlers instead of using earthen pots, which gets easily fermented in plastic bottles after a very short time and loses its nutritive values. He expressed his grief and miserable conditions of market for their product in this global era, and the way in which the fast perpetuation of global culture even into the cultural fests has resulted in the total marginalization of these artisans.

He expressed that, each of these potters have their own clients in the villages since ages as a cultural obligation. During marriages, new house ceremonies and *last right* performances these artisans have to supply the earthen pots to their clients and hence maintain their cultural significance.

He feels painful that in spite of non-biodegradable nature of plastic and steel, these are being used extensively. Though their earthen items are biodegradable and nature friendly are marginalised totally in the domestic market. Mondaiah is not aware of the global market trends or other technological advancements in pottery except *Ball-Bearing Sara*, which he wishes to have, but unfortunately non-availability is the hindrance.

He revealed that they (potters) are not aware of even a single Government Scheme meant for them exclusively, but still they are eagerly waiting for government to support them, by providing sheds for their kilns, and supplying Ball-Bearing Sara.

He works as an Agricultural Labourer to supplement his income for family expenditures during harvest and sowing seasons. He is having two sons and two daughters. His two sons are working as auto drivers, and are not interested in continuing their caste occupation which provides them very meagre income.

The case study has revealed that, the fragile nature of pottery is acting has huge hindrance for artisans to compete with plastic and steel. The food cooked in earthen utensils have huge benefits like high nutritive value, retaining hotness for long period of time, more tastier, less oil consumption, not letting the food get putrefied easily, cost effective and easily washable along with being eco-friendly in nature. In spite of all these qualities the fragile nature and heavy weight of earthenware are acting as obstacles for pottery to compete in the utilitarian market.

Case Study- 2 (Weaver)

Kundarapu Venkateshwarlu, a weaver respondent of Konne village, Bachhannapet mandal of Warangal district, at the age of 36years he along with his wife Padma actively participates in the caste occupation of weaving for their livelihood. He is having two children, son studying 9th class and daughter studying 8th class in government school.

He owns a pit loom and is an independent weaver who weaves *Pochampally silk saris* on orders. He maintains direct contact with traders who sell *pochampally saris*. The design of the saris along with the colour patterns and number of saris of each design will be decided by the trader. Venkateshwarlu will purchase raw yarn from Jangon town; he says that getting raw silk yarn is not difficult for them. But he has to invest in between Rs.16,000/- to Rs.18,000/- initially for raw yarn, dyes and soaps etc., from which they can weave nearly 8 silk saris.

According to him pre-loom activities are very laborious, time consuming, demands huge patience and immense skill during designing, colouring and setting the thread on the loom frame needs experience. The work is microscopic in nature, in long run it results in sight related problems. He says that the nuclear family cannot support the caste occupations because it becomes very difficult for women to perform both house hold and pre-loom activities. To complete the pre-loom activities it takes nearly 15 days. For maintaining the continuity of looming, by the time one lot of the yarn is on looming another lot of raw silk yarn should be undergoing pre-loom activities, for which the weaver again has to spend Rs.16,000/- to Rs.18,000/-. Hence to maintain continuity of looming, the weaver should spend around Rs.35,000/- on raw silk yarn. This financial requirement mostly forces them to make loans from money lenders, the interest of which reduces the income made from selling the silk saris.

Venkateshwarlu says, he weaves nearly 10 hours per day from morning 6AM to 6PM to avoid the power problems. He adopts traditional mode of production and weaves eight saris from one lot of raw silk yarn in a period of 45 to 60 days. The nature of work makes them suffer from *Spine* related problems after a certain age. He shared that they will always be facing marketing uncertainty if the trader rejects to purchase the saris. He will be under debt and has to face income crisis.

Venkateshwarlu shared that, for him to weave one silk sari nearly takes a week but on the power loom it can be weaved in just 2 to 3 hours, which in turn has reduced the cost of labour drastically. Unable to compete in other fabrics like cotton, polyester which are coarse in nature, most of the weavers of his region have opted to weave silk saris only, which they are proficient in and it can leave some margin for them. There are 50 weavers from his village being members in the *Sideshwara Silk Society* (Reg. body) and one Director and Co-chairman positions are allotted for their village, but there is no substantial benefit outcome from the society.

The case study has revealed that, since last 10 to 15 years the technological advancement and economic liberalization brought about by globalization has made the life of the traditional weavers miserable, who are facing extreme competition from the corporate based textile industries, which has marginalized their traditional production only towards certain fabrics like silk.

Case Study- 3 (Blacksmith)

Thangallapalli Sudarshana Chary , one of the Blacksmith respondents at Peddagundavelli Village of Dubbaka Mandal in Medak District., is not only a traditional occupational blacksmith of 66 years of age, who studied up to PUC and still opted to continue his traditional caste occupation as the caste occupation incurred reasonably good income at that period of time. He was a able blacksmith in the Dubbaka Mandal.

He makes agricultural implements for ploughing (*Karlu, Danthepalugu), sickles, tools supporting traditional water irrigation in fields, Sceptic sanchelu, axes, digging implements* etc. He used to get 24kg of paddy/Maize (*3 budlu),* under barter system, from each farmer per crop (6months).

Thangallapalli Sudarshana Chary shared that, when he was young there was plenty of work for them to do in the caste occupation, as agriculture flourished in the rural sector to a very large extent and it was traditional. They had traditional distribution relations with the farmers and they used to make and supply all the implements and tools required by the farmers for agriculture.

He says that, since last 20years the agriculture sector has undergone many changes like reduction in the agricultural production due to reduced agricultural land because of *real-estate/SEZ/Industrial Sector/Urbanization.* Apart from this modernization of agriculture, shift from food crop to cash crop production etc.

This in turn has reduced the dependence of the farmers on the traditional blacksmiths. This transformation gave a huge blow to the traditional blacksmith artisans' livelihood.

He also had welding machine to make tools and implements as for the requirements of modern trends. He adopted modern technology partially, according to his capability to face the modern demands, but still he opines that, in spite of these efforts his income is below subsistence. He is not given any electric subsidy on the welding machine. To supplement the income of the family his wife is doing *beedi rolling*.

He is having four children i.e., two daughters and two sons, two of his daughters are married, one being a school teacher and other house wife. Among his two sons, one son is working as a government school teacher and other is private lecturer. His sufficient income from traditional caste occupation prior to globalization i.e., during childhood of his children, enabled him to educate them. Now the circumstances are totally different, the income is below subsistence and to supplement the family expenditure even his wife is doing *beedi rolling.*

The case study has revealed that Indian society depended on the traditional blacksmiths since ages. But the advent of globalization has shifted the dependence of agricultural sector from traditional blacksmiths to corporate companies which not only led to total marginalization of blacksmiths but they are not even being recognized. The traditional blacksmith skill is in final stage of being wiped out completely.

5.5 Impact of Globalization

i. Pottery

The Ethnographic study made on this community has revealed that, these communities lived a self-sustainable life prior to Industrialization and enjoyed respect in the society. When the houses were not cement roofed i.e., mud tiles were used for roofing which made other communities of the village to rely on these artisans for mud tiles. These communities were busy throughout the year with hand full of work. This traditional caste occupation gave them the confidence of sustainability even in the hardest days. They enjoyed the legacy and each family had their own customers surrounding their village.

With the advent of modernization more and more families started constructing modern houses with cement roofing which gave a hard blow to the income of the community. From this period the income of caste production started decreasing because mud tile production occupied major portion of work and income for the community. The augmentation of Globalization has further increased the concrete roofing even in the rural areas, which gave a very huge blow to the caste occupation. This resulted in the traditional occupation becoming seasonal.

However, they managed their livelihood, but the advent of *plastic* and *steel* gave a death blow to the caste occupation. The cultural imperialism brought about by Globalization made the people so modern that they started performing the cultural fests like *Bonalu* using Aluminum/Bronze vessels. Though the community gets very meager income from the caste occupation even after baring of lot of drudgery, they continue to produce for maintaining and sustaining the cultural norms related to *cultural fests, gruhapraveshams, marriages and performing the 'last rights'.*

Even the seasonal *Toddy tappers* are using 'Pepsi' and 'ThumsUp' bottles for collecting *Toddy* instead of earthen pots. In spite of the fact that, Plastic and Steel are not biodegradable and cause environmental pollution right from their production process, due to their easy handling and non-breakable capability, the Steel and Plastic are giving a very tough competition to *Earthen products.*

Refrigerators (which cause ozone depletion) have become very common in the global era, resulting in the large reduction in the usage of *earthen pots* for storing and cooling water. All these factors have made the usage and production of *Earthen utensils* nearby extinction but still the community show their love, attachment and cultural obligation in continuing the traditional production, the usage of which is restricted to a few cultural norms. Potters could earn a living only if they muddy their hands with wet clay and keep steering the potter's wheel. The cultural significance and relevance of the community is retained only due to nonintervention of other communities in the production process, because of drudgery of work and very meager benefits if any.

Globalization is forcing the potters to shift to the other income sources for sustaining their livelihood. Most of these families of the ethnographic study rely on the agriculture for supplementing their family expenditure, along with maintaining the traditional production with its cultural heritage.

ii. Weavers

Before the advent of the British, India was known all over the world for its *silk and fabric production.* Prior to colonization weavers enjoyed respect in the society with huge scope of market for their fabric. During the colonial rule, the British has made many discrepancies towards the indigenous weavers, which resulted in decline of this traditional occupation.

After independence, a separate ministry was allotted for the welfare of weavers as weaving provides second highest employment after agriculture in the rural artisanal sector. So, this caste occupation to some extent finds certain government schemes / policies for promoting and marketing the production.

Since the last 10 to 15years the technological advancement and economic liberalization brought about by the globalization had adversely affected the traditional weaver in two ways. In one way, the traditional weavers' income got drastically reduced when they are competing with power-loom production, which takes very less time to weave an item and so most of the orders from temples are grabbed by the master weavers. The master weaver in turn either install their own power-looms and employ the weavers on wage basis per piece, or give sub-orders to those weavers who have their own power-looms. In another way, the traditional handloom weavers face huge competition in the market from the fabrics produced by the corporate textiles mills. These corporates which adopts the latest technology enables them to produce computerized printing saris, which not only look very much like handlooms but are also price compatible, thereby, attracting domestic customers. These made the traditional weavers not only marginalized to weave certain specific fabrics like silk, but are also hugely exploited by the intervention of the middlemen due to globalization.

The augmentation of Globalization resulted in increased import goods, technological flow making the indigenous production of handlooms to slip from the hands of traditional weavers. The various government schemes and policies meant for protecting indigenous artisans, due to low literacy of artisans, improper data and approach of government policies have become pro-trader.

This led to the intervention of middleman, i.e., traders, master weavers, deemed exporters etc., who earn more profits than the artisans in production. This intervention of the other caste communities in the production stream through power looms reduced the weaver from owner status to worker status. It has also resulted in the loss of cultural trait of the community due to the intervention of the other communities in the production.

iii. Blacksmith

The community was once called the *'Native Engineers'*. The contribution of Blacksmiths was very significant in the development of civilization. Their contribution was huge in supplying *arsenal, chariots, and huge gates for the palaces, stupas, pillars* and many more articles for kings and kingdoms apart from supplying tools and implements for farmers and other community members. The Iron victory pillar of Delhi is 23.08 feet tall and 16 inches of diameter, weighing 6.3 tons at base, is corrosion resistant since last 1700 years. The sword of *Tipu sultan* was known for its toughness due to high Carbon content, which exemplifies the skill of traditional blacksmiths. The indigenous production of *Wootz* steel made the nation world famous. The advent of British and the establishment of colonial rule have made all the efforts to wipe out the *wootz steel* and which results decline of the arsenal production.

The extinction of *Autocracy* (king's rule) and establishment of democracy has resulted in a class of artisans i.e., blacksmiths who relied hugely on kingdoms for their livelihood being marginalized, and have to completely rely on agricultural sector for their livelihood.

The augmentation of Globalization and technological advancement it brought about has mechanized the traditional agricultural production thereby snatching off the livelihood of the accommodated blacksmiths, giving death blow to the caste occupation. Once glorified blacksmiths came to road sides of urban areas, now reduce to manufacture certain cookery utensils like *chepathi, dosa pans, deep frying pans* etc. Even in this transformation they face competition from *Teflon non-stick* cookware. The intervention of other TNCs in production made them lose their cultural significance for the society. Perhaps, this might be the last generation of blacksmiths we are going to see.

The epistemology of this caste occupation is very much essential in framing the policies schemes for the safeguarding the community and their skills by the government and academic bodies.

Reference

1. www.blonnet.com.

Chapter - 6

Findings and Conclusions

In the Indian context every Artisan community has a different tradition, a different need and different capacity. These artisan communities were linked to consumer communities of the locale and had domestic markets with local demand for products.

Globalization has changed the need for localized activities and the demand for products has also changed. The objective of present study is to explore the changing caste professions in relation to women artisans in the specified locale especially for *Pottery, Weaving and Blacksmith* in the context of Globalization.

Objectives

The first objective of the study intends to analyze

(i) The Socio-Economic condition of the Artisan Caste occupations, whether Globalization has improved or deteriorated Artisans living status in general and Women Artisans in particular.

Parameters like: Income, Nature of house, Literacy, and other part time work the respondents involved in to supplement their income, were taken into consideration for understanding the socio economic status of the community.

Potters

The field study showed a poor literacy rate among this artisanal community, there is absolute illiteracy among major section of these artisanal community and very few artisans can hardly read / write. This low literacy rate acts as major hurdle for these artisans to access / avail the government schemes/policies and can hardly think of global market and their approach to it. They totally rely on their caste occupation for their sustenance and livelihood; they depend on local market only. It is noteworthy that most of the children of respondents are pursing UG/PG courses.

The empirical study has revealed that these potters can work only six months in a year i.e., from January to June. The environment is not conducive to work from July to Dec., due to prevailing wet conditions in Rainy and Winter seasons. The Potter Caste profession is surviving very little extent due to prevailing Cultural practices of the society in the global era, the survival of this caste profession is comparatively louder nearby Shiva temples, though now a days the devotees are offering *Bonalu* in metallic vessels which cause a serious threat to the survival of potter caste occupation and also serious aberration in the cultural practice as per Hindu mythology. The study clearly reflects the marginalization of these artisanal products in the wake of globalization, pushing these traditional artisans to adverse poverty.

These artisans continue the caste profession even in odd times and are responsible for the survival of the caste profession under Cultural Economy. Due to low marketable opportunities in global era, they engage in other part-timeworks to supplement their income. They are working as agricultural labourers, *RojagarYojana* workers, Auto/Private Bus driver, women in the family actively participate in caste profession along the *beedi rolling* work. Some have no scope to do any other work due to their age factor but practice the caste profession as self-esteem.

The rural artisans income in this global era is hand to mouth, miserable living conditions are prevailing among the traditional artisans of pottery who are not only maintaining and perpetuating the artisanal skill of production along with cultural heritage but are also sustaining the cultural significance of the society.

The low socio-economic status of the traditional pottery artisans was reflected in the empirical study, demanding an exigency of policy maker's attention for upholding and protecting these traditional cultural expressions of the artisans in the global era.

Role of the Women

In the traditional family based production the role of the women is indispensable. Women play an extremely important role in following phases of production,

1. Beating the clay
2. Soaking the clay
3. Fine segregation of the clay
4. Constructing a small banking for soaked clay and adding ash of the kiln to make clay hard and soft.
5. Drying the utensils in shadow.
6. Watching the kiln to maintain temperature for 4 hours for baking.
7. Most importantly, local marketing.

Women play an important role, without their support it is not possible to carry the production. In these family based home productions every member of the family right from children of 6 years age to the aged family members who can walk contribute in production according to their capability.

Weavers

The field studies revealed that majority of these artisans are having secondary level literacy, i.e enough to read / write, but cannot represent themselves. Very small section of the community has absolute illiteracy. This low literacy becomes a huge hurdle for these artisans to avail the various government schemes meant for them. The empirical study has revealed that, however these artisans are able to avail few government welfare schemes to some extent. As this artefact sector has a separate ministry at central government level, many efforts by the government seem to be taken to protect and promote these artisans. But empirical study reveals that at the gross root level the artisans are able to access only pension and scholarships to their children, they are not even aware of most of the government schemes which are ultimately slipping through the cracks in policies in to the middlemen hands.

The poor educational qualifications clearly reflect their poor economic conditions, but interestingly they put maximum efforts in educating their children. Most of the children of respondents are pursuing Under graduate and Post graduate programmes, some are pursuing for TTC and B.Ed. courses.

The empirical study revealed that majority of these artisans are *handloom* weavers and some are *power loom* weavers. The Handloom weavers are prone to work only 6 months in a year i.e., from January to June. The environment is not conducive to work from the month of July to December, due to prevailing wet conditions in *Rainy* and *winter* seasons. Whereas Power loom weavers can work throughout the year provided, they get work orders from master weaver. But they are also facing the Electric Power cut problems during the months of February to May every year.

The field study shows, most of weavers are (handloom weavers) having their annual income in the range of Rs. 10,001 – Rs. 25,000/-, some of handloom weavers has an annual income between Rs. 25,001/- to Rs. 40,000/- as they have trade links with traders / master weavers of silk. Not even a single handloom weaver respondent is able to earn above Rs. 40,000/-. The handloom weavers are more vulnerable to market risks and price fluctuations in procuring raw material. In Telangana region, mostly the handloom weavers indulge in production of silk saris, *pochampally* saris and cotton saris.

The weavers who are operating power looms get their orders from master weavers, who are basically contractors and capable of availing both Centre and State Government schemes/policies and these weavers get payment as piece meal process. Due to the availability of Electric power subsidy up to 50% on the total consumption, 12% of total respondents (75%of power loom weavers) having their annual income above Rs. 40,000/-. But they are also facing two important problems namely, *repairs of looms, non-payment of bills from master weaver in timely*. The weavers having power looms are to some extent free from direct market risks and price fluctuations for raw material due to master weaver presence. So, majority of the handloom weavers are shifting towards power looms. Since power looms are not easily available in the market and have repairing problems, these handloom weavers are becoming power loom workers under the master weavers. Hence, under globalization, owners are more vulnerable to become workers for sustaining.

As these artisans are having their annual income below Rs. 40,000/- from their caste occupation, these weavers are engaged in other part-time works to supplement their income. They are working in power looms as wage workers, working at cloth merchant shops, women do *beedi rolling* work.

The rural weaver artisans' income in this global era is only hand to mouth which clearly reflects the low socio economic condition of this artisanal community. Miserable conditions are prevailing among the traditional artisans who are maintaining and perpetuating cultural identity and heritage of this region. In spite of their love and passion towards caste occupation, they are not interested to make their children continue the same caste profession and live in misery.

Role of Women

The role of women in the traditional family based caste production is requisite. Processing yarn, Pre-loom activities are done by women, they maintain processed yarn readily available for the continuity of looming, and looming is also done by some women weavers. Women play an important role, without their support it is not possible to carry the production

Aged persons and school dropouts if any make their contributions according to their capacity. Handloom by nature supports only optimum size families. It can neither support a 'nuclear type of family' nor does it support a 'big joint family'. In almost all the home based handloom production each member of the family makes their contribution according to their ability.

Designing and looming are generally done by men, as the nature of work demands more physical strength and concentration. By the time weaving of one lot yarn is finished there should be another processed lot of yarn readily available for continuity of looming.

The ethnographic study reveals that in globalization modern means of production i.e power-loom production has totally marginalized women.

Blacksmiths

The empirical study revealed very low literacy rate among this artisanal community, there is absolute illiteracy among major section of these artisanal community and very few artisans can hardly read / write. In this era of globalization life of blacksmiths became nomadic; they migrate to different regions for their livelihood, so most of the children of respondents are not pursing education seriously.

The majority of blacksmiths are having their work from onset of agricultural activities. When agriculture was purely traditional base, they used to get work in preparing *Karllu, Dhantheypalugu, Sickels, Water rings Sanchelu, Sceptic Sanchelu etc.*

The blacksmiths are prone to work only 6 to 8 months in a year. The Blacksmith profession is hardly surviving in the advent of modernization of Agriculture and machine made kitchenware in the globalized era. They are becoming semi-nomadic and slowly losing their cultural identity in the society. Probably, this generation may be the last generation in performing this caste occupation, due to low marketable opportunities, they engage part-timely on other works. Their annual income is generally below Rs.15,000/-, to supplement their income some blacksmiths engage in other part-time works. These artisans are performing welding works or carpentry works to supplement their income, some artisans have to scope to do any other work due to their age factor and perform only their caste profession.

It was also observed during fieldwork that, the number of working blacksmiths within a village can range widely from two to three only. However, overall the number of working smithies is rapidly declining since younger generations are opting to work as rod benders in building constructions, as welders, fitters and join the companies making grills or car tinkering workshops.

The empirical study has shown that the technological advancement brought about by the globalization has totally brought the blacksmith artisans to a dead-end by transforming their livelihood into the pockets of corporate companies.

Role of Women

Generally in traditional mode of production which was done in Sheds, women were not allowed in the smithy, but in this era of globalization the situations have altered their life styles and production became family based, women now contribute in the production and perform works like *collecting coal, Gannu beating, blowing air, Marketing the products by carrying to the local markets, fairs or to houses in local.*

The second objective of study intends to understand

(ii) Trace the relation of Globalization with regard to accommodation / resistance towards the transformation of Artisan Caste Professions.

Parameters like: Age, Tools, Raw material, Articles made, Working Hours, Outside Employees, Price, Number of clients, Power requirements, Financial requirements, Repairs, Market constraints etc. have been taken into consideration for analyzing the above objective.

Potters

With the advent of industrialization in 19th century, slowly changes started taking place in technology. Technology that comes from time to time has introduced a whole range of vessels and household utensils that were supplied by potters in traditional India. The pottery is gradually being marginalized from the mainframe utility items at the household level even in many villages.

The situation became worst when the *mud roof tiles* were replaced by concrete roofing, which reduced total demand for *mud roof tiles* and much of the livelihood of these communities became miserable. The excessive usage of plastic gave a death blow to the community livelihood. Consequently, it is self-evident that, potters being marginalized i.e., a section of skilled artisanal population being left without their livelihood opportunities.

Apart from this, in the wake of modernity and globalization, the plastic vases and cement vases are replacing mud vases in gardens; even these vases are given red colour to give look of mud vases, giving a tough competition to mud vases. It is evident from market trend for past two to three years that electric lamps in small plastic pans looking like Diyas being replaced to original Clay Diyas.

From technology concern the only tool that the potters identified with is '*a potter's wheel* ', called as "*Sara*". Indian government agencies like Khadi and Village Industries Commission (KVIC) along with international agencies United Nations Development Programme (UNDP) have extended support and helped introduce a whole range of improved tools, machines and technology in pottery which includes Buck Machine, Ball Mill, Power-run-potter's wheel, Jigger Machine, Gas Chula and so on. These are of course acquired by organized potters only.

As pottery, in Telangana region is rural-based artisanal caste occupation, which is basically unorganized. As most of the potters are less educated they are unaware of these improved tools and do not get such support, but they have no regret for non-availability of these improved tools. They look forward from the government to have loan for construction of work-shed or shed for the kiln where they bake the pottery articles in order to protect the articles from sudden rain, and a bearing *sara*(potter's wheel which runs on ball bearing not on power).

The reasons for Telangana potters not so curious about the latest machinery could be

(i) Machineries not user friendly
(ii) Maintenance of which unknown to potters (they cannot repair defects)

(iii) Machines remain unused for long time for non-availability of repairing parts/mechanic may get rusted.

(iv) Extra financial burden to purchase new machineries which may be costly comparatively to traditional one.

(v) More space requirement for keeping these machineries.

(vi) New machineries lead to more production, thereby pressurizing potter to market. As the market is already reduced, this may lead stock accumulation. This once again requires space to keep the stock protected, as the articles are delicate.

Change in the mindset of the people has resulted in poor off-take of pottery articles and poor income to the potters, except in few places where still local cultures remain undisturbed like in Kerala and Kanyakumari.

The potters are aware of the fact that the market and modernity are marginalizing the pottery tradition and the demand for ethnic items. The increasing role of fashion trends and market dynamics keep silently communicating to the potters that they should turn to doing red pottery articles and terracotta items only for the antique shops in five star hotels, and not for any utilitarian value as it used to be with women in traditional kitchens.

This artisanal community production is prominently sustain near the *Shiva Temples* due to cultural form of *Bonalu* in *Earthen Pots* in the regions of Telangana i.e., *Raja Rajeshwari Temple*, Vemulawada of Karimnagar district, *Rekula Kunta Mallana Temple,* near Terlumadi village, Mustabad Mandal of Karimnagar district, *Mallikarjunaswamy Temple*, near Kummargudem of Mallikudurla village, Dharmasagar Mandal of Warangal district, *Kommuravelli Mallanna Temple*, near Kommuravelli village, Cheryala Mandal, of Warangal district.

The field study clearly indicates that the younger generations of these artisanal (potters) communities are not showing much interest in performing traditional caste occupation, in the global era due to market constraints.

Weavers

The ethnographic study revealed that, era of globalization led to the extinction of joint family system, which made it very difficult for women to cope with works of caste production (processing of yarn, & pre loom activities) along with child rearing & caring, the situation becomes even worse.

Encroachment of power loom in to the hand loom sector is that certain orders meant specifically for handlooms are procured by master weavers of power looms, who execute the order carried out in power looms with a tag attached to it as "Handloom product". This is prevalent not only in domestic market sales, but also in export items.The deemed exporters although are aware of it.

Most of the handloom weavers of Telangana region are weaving silk. As silk is soft and could be weaved with comparatively less physical strain when compared with cotton cloth which gives meager income. So weavers of Telangana in general and rural weavers in particular have given up cotton weaving and weave silk saris only.

Fabric like cotton, polyester are weaved on power looms, based on the item being weaved i.e., towels, bed sheets, saris and lounges different power looms are used. The size of power loom in length varies depending on items woven. So, with the advent of globalization the hand loom weavers of Telangana have restricted to silk saree weaving only. Some of the weavers have accommodated to power loom production, and artisans who are not able to withstand the drudgery of traditional work due to nuclear family structure, who have financial crisis in adopting and maintaining modern technology and who cannot with stand the market competition became workers in the industrial cooperatives .There is huge exploitation due the intervention of the middlemen in the form of master weaver / trader in the wake of globalization.

The field study has revealed that, since last 10 to 15 years the technological advancement and economic liberalization brought about by globalization has made the life of the traditional weavers miserable, who are facing extreme competition from the corporate based textile industries, which has marginalized their traditional production only towards certain fabrics like silk.

The empirical study shows a declining trend towards continuing caste profession among the younger generations of weaving community due to various constraints with the advent of globalization.

Blacksmiths

The Modernization of agriculture in the global era has drastically brought down the tools and implements. Instead of traditional bullock carts and tools, tractors and machineries are increasingly used for farming. This made the agricultural implements and tool production to slip from the traditional blacksmith artisan's hands into the hands of big factories.

The repair of tire wheels is attended to by an Automobile workshop and not by traditional blacksmiths. Tractor replaced bullock carts, thereby no bullocks required for pulling carts which made the horse-shoe nail demand die out, a product slipped from the hands of traditional blacksmiths. This situation made the blacksmiths nomadic with less work at hand; they have to migrate to different regions (urban) for livelihood. They make their living by repairing iron tools and implements like Sickle, Axe, Spade, Knife, and Knife sharpening for the local people.

The augmentation of Globalization and technological advancement it brought about has mechanized the traditional agricultural production thereby snatching off the livelihood of the accommodated blacksmiths, giving death blow to the caste occupation. Once glorified blacksmiths came to road sides of urban areas, now reduce to manufacture certain cookery utensils like *chepathi, dosa pans, deep frying pans* etc. Even in this transformation they face competition from *Teflon non-stick* cookware. The intervention of other TNCs in production made them lose their cultural significance for the society.

The ethnographic study reflects an extreme decreased trend of practicing the caste profession among the younger generations of this artisanal community. The younger generations are not interest in continuing this occupation. Perhaps, this might be the last generation of blacksmiths we are going to witness.

The third objective of study is to

(iii) Explore the cultural significance, hidden scientific and eco-friendly nature of indigenous Artisanal Caste production.

Parameters like: Cultural obligation, Scientific and ecofriendly nature of production, Health concerns of the community, Form of support they expect, were taken to have a holistic understanding of the indigenous Artisanal Caste production.

Potters

The huge cultural significance of this artisanal production to the community was profoundly evident in the field study.

Cultural Significance

The potters' community maintains its cultural significance to the society in general and during the following occasions in particular.

(i) during birth (presently practice extinguished)

(ii) during marriages

(iii) Gruhapraveshams

(iv) Cultural fests like *Bonalu*

(v) Death ceremony including carrying ash to sacred rivers

Potters continue their caste occupations basically for maintaining the cultural significance of the society. They, in all circumstances always provide their clients with pottery items when asked for.

Environment Friendly

They are biodegradable, does not pollute the environment through wastages in production. The entire process of making the pottery is environmental friendly process.

Benefits of Earthen cook-ware

(i) The nutrient value of food cooked in earthen ware is rich, tastier, keeps the food hot for longer time and preserves the food longer time without being putrefied.

(ii) The food items like *tamarind, items rich in vitamin-C,* when cooked in steel /Aluminum vessels will undergo chemical reaction, whereas the same items cooked in the *earthen vessels* will not undergo such reactions.

(iii) If food cooked in *earthen vessels* gets over fried, the burnt flavor will not percolate to entire dish.

(iv) Oil consumption for cooking in pottery vessels after 2/3 times usage will be very less.

(v) Pottery utensils will be excellent for storing pickles and also increase the flavor.

(vi) The food cooked in *earthen vessels* remains hot for long time.

Since they are delicate, need to be handled carefully and can be cleaned easily.

Health Issues of these artisans

The persons involved in pottery occupation prone to Backache, Knee problems, Respiratory problems. They consume *tamarind soup* frequently to get rid of respiratory problems caused by fine clay dust. A person once medically operated is unfit to perform the caste occupation. Skidding of the *Sara* from the pivot causes severe injuries to legs during molding the clay.

Weavers

Cultural Significance

The intervention of middleman who belongs to other caste communities, in the form of traders, master weavers, deemed exporters etc., to earn more profits than the artisans in production, has resulted in the loss of cultural trait of the community. So, the field study could not trace the cultural Significance of this community to the society due to the intervention of other castes & corporate sectors in the production process.

Environment Friendly

The traditional mode of looming is ecofriendly in nature, detergents and the dyes used for processing the yarn and the pre loom activities in the traditional based artisanal production does not cause harm to the nature ,but the corporate mode of textile production causes air and water pollution.

Health Issues of these artisans

1. The handloom weavers suffer from spine related problems due to their compulsion to sit for long hours nearly 10 hours per day for weaving on the loom without any back support.
2. Due to microscopic nature of work they suffer from sight problems after certain age, which hampers their ability to perform the caste occupation.
3. Pre-loom activities of Boiling, cleaning and dyeing may cause serious lung infections and lung related diseases due to pungent smell, smoke and chemicals of dyeing in long run.
4. Power looms are not as safer as traditional looms i.e., the safety and security of power looms is less comparatively. The workers of power looms are not covered by handloom insurance.

Blacksmith

Cultural Significance

Indian farmers in traditional agriculture used tools such as plough, spade, sickle and a pair of bullock for ploughing. Blacksmiths and Carpenters used to provide and repair all these tools/implements required for farming. There was a caste based interdependency among these communities.

Mammayee Festival was celebrated by blacksmiths as a mark of renewal of ritual contract for a long-standing relationship with the farming community.

The nomadic/semi-nomadic mode of life of the blacksmiths in global era, and the intervention of other castes in the production process through TNCs has resulted in the loss of cultural significance of this community to the society.

Environment Friendly

In the traditional mode of production the blacksmith community has the technology of extracting metals from ores, smelting and producing char coal without causing much harm to the environment. But this epistemology has been gradually lost to a very large extent.

Whereas, the modern mode of production in not eco-friendly, it causes huge pollution to air, water and extinction of resources.

Health Issues of these artisans

As the nature of work demands huge physical strength, they get more physically strained by the end of the day and to relieve themselves from body pains they habituated to alcohol of cheap quality liquor, which results in adverse chronic diseases.

Hypothesis

In the Artisanal Caste occupations family acts as an Economic unit, production process demands complete co-operation of the family at home based production without gender discrimination. *'Artisan' refers equal footing for male and female i.e., gender free.*

The first Hypothesis is

(i) Global means of communication and information greatly contribute to the choices of profession. Augmentation of Technological advancement alters the Caste professions in the Globalization era.

Potters

This hypothesis had been accepted through the empirical study.

Globalization is forcing the potters to shift to the other income sources for sustaining their livelihood. Most of these families of the ethnographic study rely on the agriculture for supplementing their family expenditure, along with maintaining the traditional production as a cultural heritage.

Weavers

This Hypothesis was accepted through the empirical study.

The technological advancement and economic liberalization brought about by the globalization had adversely affected the traditional weaver in two ways. In one way it resulted in drastic reduction of the income of traditional weavers when they are competing with power-loom production, which are cost effective and take very less time and effort to weave an item and so most of the orders grabbed by the master weavers. The master weaver in turn either install their own power-looms and employ the weavers on wage basis per piece, or give sub-orders to those weavers who have their own power-looms. In another way, the traditional handloom weavers face huge competition in the market from the fabrics produced by the corporate textiles mills. These corporates which adopts the latest technology enables them to produce computerized printing saris, which not only look very much like handlooms but are also price compatible, thereby, attracting domestic customers. These made the traditional weavers not only marginalized to weave certain specific fabrics like silk, but are also hugely exploited by the intervention of the middlemen due to globalization.

Blacksmiths

This Hypothesis was accepted through the empirical study.

With the advent of globalization, the agriculture sector has undergone many changes like reduction in the agricultural production due to reduced agricultural land because of *real-estate/SEZ/Industrial Sector/Urbanization*. Apart from this modernization of agriculture, shift from food crop to cash crop production etc, have reduced the dependence of the farmers on the traditional blacksmiths. This transformation gave a huge blow to the traditional blacksmith artisans' livelihood.

Modern manufacturing technological advancement is rendering blacksmith skills obsolete.

Known for their skills since 300 AD blacksmiths of Telangana had a glorious past, the trade is in danger of being wiped out completely. Extreme poverty of traditional blacksmiths due to very less work at hand is forcing these artisans to shift to other works for livelihood, which not only affects the social fabric but also leads to artefact diminishing (loss of skill).

The Second Hypothesis generated was

(ii) In Globalization, even accommodated caste professions are not being able to withstand Market economy.

Potters

In the light of the data generated in the study the Hypothesis was approved.

With the advent of modernization and construction of modern houses with cement roofing which gave a hard blow to the income of the community. From this period the income of caste production started decreasing because mud tile production occupied major portion of work and income for the community. Globalization has further percolated the concrete roofing even to the rural areas, which gave a very huge blow to the caste occupation. This resulted in the traditional occupation becoming seasonal.

However, they managed their livelihood; excessive use of *plastic* and *steel utensils* gave a death blow to the caste occupation. The cultural imperialism brought about by Globalization made the people so modern that they started performing the cultural fests like *Bonalu* using Aluminum/ Bronze vessels. Replacement of earthen pots with plastic pots for planting, using electric diyas during fests like Deepavali has totally marginalized these artisanal communities.

Even the seasonal *Toddy tappers* are using 'Pepsi' and 'ThumsUp' bottles for collecting *Toddy* instead of earthen pots. In spite of the fact that, Plastic and Steel are not biodegradable and cause environmental pollution right from their production process, due to their easy handling and non-breakable capability, the Steel and Plastic are giving a very tough competition to *Earthen products.*

Though the community gets very meager income from the caste occupation even after baring lot of drudgery, they continue to produce for maintaining and sustaining the cultural norms related to *cultural fests, gruhapraveshams, marriages and performing the 'last rights'.*

Weavers

This hypothesis was accepted in the light of the data generated in the empirical study.

The augmentation of Globalization resulted in increased import goods, technological flow making the indigenous production of handlooms to slip from the hands of traditional weavers. The various government schemes and policies meant for protecting indigenous artisans, due to low literacy of artisans, improper data and approach of government policies have become pro-trader.

This led to the intervention of middleman, i.e., traders, master weavers, deemed exporters etc., who earn more profits than the artisans in production.

Blacksmiths

In the light of the data generated in the study the Hypothesis is accepted. Industrial Revolution has restricted the blacksmith community to the manufacturing of tools/implements for farmers; they sustained their livelihood by this caste interdependence. But the technological advancement of globalization has modernized agriculture sector and reduced the agriculture land, forcing these artisans to shift to manufacturing of cook ware for their sustenance, where once again they face competition from the TNCs manufacturing non-stick cook ware. Hence in the global era, the blacksmith artisanal community is not able to accommodate themselves and withstand the market economy.

The Third Hypothesis posited was

(iii) Globalization hampers the Artisans and caste profession by altering the owners into workers.

Potters

The utilitarian based artisanal production of the pottery community is not able to withstand the competition of corporate Steel *and Plastic* utilitarian production due to their fragile nature, price, and weight, along with the changing trends in consumer culture in the wake of Globalization.

Though the usage and production of *earthen utensils* are nearing extinction but still the community show their love, attachment and cultural obligation in continuing the traditional production, the usage of which is restricted to a few cultural norms. Potters could earn a living only if they muddy their hands with wet clay and keep steering the potter's wheel. The cultural significance and relevance of the community is retained only due to nonintervention of other communities in the production process, because of drudgery of work and very meager benefits if any.

Most of these artisans work as agricultural labourers, rojgar yojana works, auto/ bus drivers and women involve in *beedi rolling* work to supplement their income. Globalization has altered these artisans from owners to workers.

Weavers

In the light of the data generated, the Hypothesis was accepted.

The master weavers give sub-orders to those weavers who have their own power looms, weavers purchase second hand power looms from Surat, Mumbai and Bewandi for a cost ranging between Rs. 50,000 to 1,00,000 depending on the length of power loom. Most weavers face financial crisis to purchase and maintain the power loom (for repairing). So mostly master weavers employ the power looms and employ the weavers' .This intervention of the other caste communities in the production stream through power looms reduced the weaver from owner status to worker status.

Blacksmiths

In the light of the data generated, the Hypothesis was accepted.

Globalization altered agriculture sector to a very large extent, which gave a death blow to the sustenance of traditional blacksmith, however though they managed their livelihood through manufacturing cook ware; even here they face huge competition from TNCs manufacturing non-stick cook ware. This marginalization of traditional blacksmith community has altered the blacksmith artisans from owners to workers in globalization. They are working as rod blenders, welders, fitters and join the companies making grills, or as car tinkering workshops etc.

CONCLUSIONS

Potters

Both technological advancement and the cultural Imperialism in the wake of Globalization has marginalized the usage and production of *earthen utensils* to a very large extent but the indigenous artisanal community still show their love, attachment and cultural obligation in continuing the traditional production.

The cultural significance and the relevance of the community is retained only due to non-intervention of other communities in the production process because of the drudgery of work and marginal profits if any.

Weavers

The augmentation of Globalization resulted in increased technological flow and import of goods making the indigenous production of handlooms to slip from the hands of traditional weavers. This led to the intervention of middleman in the form of traders, master weavers, deemed exporters, who belong to other caste communities and earn more profits than the artisans who produce. It has resulted in the loss of the cultural significance of this artisanal community to the society.

Blacksmith

With the advent of Globalization and the technological advancement brought about by it has totally marginalized the blacksmith artisanal community. Perhaps this might be the last generation of blacksmiths that we are going to witness as these artisans are shifting to other works for their livelihood. Wiping out of a traditional artisanal skill which has been developed since ages and perpetuated through civilizations will definitely have an adverse impact on the society as it disturbs the social fabric of the nation and also leads to loss of an indigenous skill (artifact diminishing).

In a nut shell, loss of conventional wisdom, i.e., hidden knowledge skill of traditional system being eroded slowly as it is oral and is not preserved in written form. The epistemology of these traditional artisanal communities is very much essential in framing the policies/schemes for safeguarding the artisanal communities and their skill by academic bodies and the government before they become extinct unable to bear the vicissitudes of the forces of Globalization.

Bibliography

Abraham, T.M., (1964), *Handicrafts in India*, New Delhi : graphics Columbia.

Albrow, M., (1997), *The global age : State and Society Beyond Modernity* (Stanford, CA: Stanford Univ. Press.

Arjun Appadurai, *Globalization*, Duke University, Press (2001).

Arjun Appadurai, *Disjunction and Differences in Global Cultural Economy*, In Featherstone, M., ed.: *Global Culture, Nationalism, Globalization and Modernity : A Theory, Culture and Society*, Special Issue, Sage publications, London, 1990.

Arthashastra, (2), by Kautilya.Ed.by R. Shama Sastri, 1919, pp 58-9.

Asha Krishnakumar, *Caste and the Census*, Volume 17 - Issue 18, Sept., 02 - 15, 2000, Frontline, India's National Magazine, from the publishers of The Hindu.

Aryan, S., *Craft of Himachal Pradesh*, Mapin Publishing Ahmedabad, India, 1993.

Ayush Yadav, *Globalization and Its impact on Indian Economy: Developments and Challenges*, www.legalservicesindia.com, ISBN: 978-81-928510-1-3.

AIACA and ACCESS Development Services, *Artistic Textiles of Nagaland: Diagnostic Study and Business Development plan,* ww.aiacaonline.org

Bailey, F. G., (1957), *Caste and the Economic Frontiers : A Village in High land Orissa*, Manchester, Manchester University Press.

Balasubramaniam, R (2000), "*Delhi Iron Pillar : New Insights*, Indian Institute of Advanced Studies, ISBN-81-7305-223-9.

Basu, S., The Carpet Makers, 14th August, 2005, The Hindu (Sunday Magazine).

Bayly Susan, *Caste, Society and Politics in India from the Eighteenth Century to the Modern Age*, New Cambridge History of India. Cambridge: Cambridge University Press; 1999.

Berger, Peter., Heidemann, Frank, *"The Modern Anthropology of India:Ethnography, Themes and Theory"*, Routledge, p.128, ISBN: 9781134061112.

Berman, Jan, (1974), Patronage and Exploitation: Changing Agrarian Relations in South Gujarat, India, Berkelely, California: University of California Press.

Beteille, Andre. 1992, *The Backward Classes in Contemporary India*, Delhi: Oxford University Press.

Bhagavadgita, iv, 13.

Bhagirath Lal Das, *An Introduction to Globalization and its Impacts*, Chapter-4, p. 14, TWN Global Economic Series 3, Published by Third World Network, ISBN: 983-9747-72-X.

Bharati, Ke. Ara (2001), *Chamba Himalaya: Amazing Land, Unique Culture*, Indus Publishing p.178 ISBN978-8-17387-125-2.

Bhattachan Krishan B., (2008), *Indigenous people & Minorities of Nepal*, Nepal Federation of Indigenous Nationalities (NEFIN), P. 49

Bhattarai, Hari Prasad (2004), *"Cultural Diversity and pluralism in Nepal: Emerging Issues and the Search for a New Pardigm"*, Contributions to Nepalese Studies, p-339.

"Bihar Staff to wear Khadi twice a Week", July 17th,2015, *The Hans India* English daily.

Bourdieu, Pierre, Distinction: A Social Critique of the Judgment of Taste, Translated by R. Nice. London: Routeledge. Original edition, 1979.

Chadha, G.K., (1997), *Access of Rural Households to Non-farm employment: Trends, constraints and possibilities*, in G.K. Chedha and Alakh N Sharma (eds), Op Cit., pp. 184-215.

Chatterjee Partha, *Caste and Subaltern Consciousness*, In: Guha R, editor, Subaltern Studies: Writings on South Asian History and Society. Delhi: Oxford University Press; 1992.

Chattopadhyay, Kamaladevi, (1976), *The Glory of Indian Handicrafts*, New Delhi :India Book Company.

Commander Simon, *The Jajmani System in North India: An Examination of Its Logic and Status across Two Centuries,* Modern Asian Studies. 1983; 17(2): 283–311.

Constitution of India, Part-III, *Fundamentals Rights* n. 17. http://www.culturalindia.net/indian-crafts/indian-pottery.html

Das, Veena (1982), *Structure and Cognition : Aspects of Hindu Castes and Rituals*, Bombay: Manohar.

Dasra, *Catalyst for Social Change, Report on Crafts,* January, 2013, p. 15-25.

Dantwala M.L., *India's Progress in Agrarian Reforms*, Far Eastern Survey, 1950; 19(22)

Deshpande, S., and Deshpance, L., (1998), *Impact of Liberalisation on Labour Market in India, what Facts from NSSO's 50th Round Show?*, Economic and Political Weekly, 33(2), L31-40.

Deshpande, Ashwini (2000),*Does Caste Still Define Disparity? A Look at Inequality in Kerala*, India, The American Economic Review 90 (2): 322-325.

Dirks Nicholas, *Castes of Mind: Colonialism and the Making of Modern India*,Princeton, NJ: Princeton University Press; 2001.

Doshi S. L., Post Modern Perspective on Indian Society, Rawat Publications.

Doshi, S. L., and Jain P. C., *Rural Sociology*, Rawat Publications.

Dr. Ambedkar, B.R., *Writings and Speeches*, Vol.1.part 1, Bombay: Education Department, Government of Maharashtra, 1979, pp. 3-22, Edited by Frances W. Pritchett.

Dube, S.C., *Indian Village,* Foreword by Morris E. Opler Ithaca: CornellUniversity Press, 1955.

Dumont, Louis, *Homo Hierarchicus: The Caste System and Its Implications*, Chicago: University of Chicago Press; 1980.

Edgerton *et.al.*, (2002), *"Indian and Oriental Arms and Armour"*, Courier Dover Publications, ISBN-0-486—42229-1.

Edwin Bryant, *Quest for the Origins of Vedic Culture*, 2001: pp. 211-212. Ellowood, Wayne, (2005), *The No Non-Sense Guide to Globalization*, New Delhi: Rawat Publication.

Fick, R., *Social Organization in North-East India in Buddha's Time*(trans. By Maitra), 1920, pp 32, 180-1,196-7, 255, 276, 278.

Fisher, T., Mahajan, V., and Singha, A., (1997), *The Forgotten Sector*, Intermediate Technology Publications London, p 274.

Francis Abraham M., *Contemporary Sociology*, Oxford University Press.

Friedman, Thomas, (1999), *Dueling Globalisation : A debate between Thomas Friedman and Ignacio Ramonet – DOS capital*, Foreign Policy, Fall, pp 110-127.

Friedman, Thomas, (2006), *The World is Flat : The Globalised World in Twenty-First Century*, New Delhi : Penguin.

Fukuyama, Francis. The End of History and the Last Man, New York: Free Press, 1992.

Gadgil, D. R., *Women in the Work Force in India*, Asia Publishing House, Bombay, 1965; pp 33.

Gauthama, Dharmasutra (Buhler's trans. In SBE, 1879) pp. 211, 229, 234, as per Caste and Race in India by G. S. Ghurye.

Gerth Hans, Mills C Wright. From *Max Weber: Essays in Sociology*, New York: Oxford University Press; 1946.

Ghurye, G.S., (1961 : 43) , *Caste and Race in India* , Popular Prakashan Pvt. Ltd, ISBN 978-81-7154-205-5.

"GI Tag Fails to help Venkatagiri Sari", June 29th 2015,*The Hans India* English daily.

Giddens, Anthony, *The Consequences of Modernity*, Cambridge: Polity, 1990.

Gommans, Jos J.L., (2002), *"Mughal Warfare : Indian Frontiers and Highroads to Expire 1500-1700"*, Routledge, ISBN 0-415-23989-3.

Gough Kathleen, *Rural Society in Southeast India*, Cambridge Studies in Social Anthropology, Cambridge: Cambridge University Press; 1981.

Gould, Roger V, (2002), *The Origins of Status Hierarchies : A Formal Theory and Empherical Test*, American Journal of Sociology, 107(5); 1143-1178.

Grusky, David B., Manwai C Ku, and Szoonja Szelenyi, eds. 2008, *Social Stratification : Class, Race and Gender in Sociological Perspective*, Bowlder: Westview Press.

Gupta, Dipankar, (2005), *Caste and Politics: Identity Over System*, Annual Review of Anthropology 34: 409-427.

Heather L. Ross and Isabel V. Sawhill , *The family as Economic Unit,* The Wilson Quarterly / Winter 1977.

Heileiner, Eric.,*Alternatives to Neoliberalism?*in: Stubs, Richard and Geoffrey Underhill. Political Economy and the Changing Global Order, Oxford: Oxford University Press, 2006.

Held, David and Anthony Mc Grew, *Globalization Theory: Approaches and Controversies*, Polity, 2007.

Hezell, P.B.R., and Haggblade, S., *Rural Growth Linkages in India*, Indian Journal of Agricultural Economics, 46(4), pp. 515-29.

Hopkins, H.G., (2002), *Introduction : Globalization – An Agenda for Historians*, in A. G. Hopkins (Ed), Globalization in World History, London : Pimlico, pp. 1-10.

Hirst, Paul and Thompson, Grahame, *The Limits to Economics Globalization*, in: Held, David and Anthony McGrew, *The Global Transformations Reader: An Introduction to the Globalization Debate*, Polity, 2003. http://busines.mapsofindia.com/indiaindstry/pottery.html

Huntington, Samuel, *The Clash of Civilizations and the Remaking of World Order*, New York: Simon & Schuster, 1996.

Hutton, J. H. Caste, Undergraduate Review, Vol. 13, Issue. 1 (2001), Art. 4, in *India: Its Nature, Function, and Origins*. Oxford: Oxford UP, 1963.

India, Science and Technology, S&T for *Rural India and Inclusive growth 2008*, http://www.nistads.res.in

"India's legendary Wootz steel", Material Engineering division, IISc, Banglore.

Jaitly J, *Visvakarma's Children : Stories of India's Craft people, 2001*, Published by AK Mittal, Concept publishing company, New Delhi, ISBN:81-7022-895-6

Jawaharlal Nehru, *The Discovery of India*, Jawaharlal Nehru memorial fund, New Delhi, Oxford University Press, 1982, p. 298.

Jena P.K., *Orissan Handicrafts in the Age of Globalization: Threats and Opportunities*, in Mukherjee D, Indian Handlooms and Handicrafts : Issues and Experiences, 2009.

John Williamson, *Globalization: The Concept, Causes, and Consequences*, as Key note address as Chief Economist for the South Asia Region at the World Bank, 15th Dec., 1998.

Johnson L, *Legal Structures for community – owned enterprises*, presentation at LEAD Workshop, Ahmedabad, 2011.

Kamaladevi Chettopadyay, *Handicrafts of India*, 2nd edn, Indraprastha Press,New Delhi, 1985.

"Karnataka State Gazetteer : Belgaum", printed by the Director of Print Stationery and publications at the Govt. press.

Karve, Irawati, (1953), *Kinship Organization in India*, Poona, Deccan College Monograph Series.

Keshav Chandra Gupta ,*Progress and Prospects of Pottery industry in India: A case study of U.P.*, Mittal Publications, pp 18 – ISBN 978-81-7099-051-2.

Khare, R.S., *The Untouchable's Version: Evaluating an Ideal Ascetic*, In: Gupta D, editor. Social Stratification. New Delhi: Oxford University Press; 1991

Konenda, Puline (1997), *Caste in Contemporary India : Beyond Organic Solidarity*, Jaipur, India, Rawat Publications.

Kothari C.R., *Research Methodology Methods and Techniques,* New Age International Publishers.

Kumar, Anand, (2009), "*Sociology and the Challenges of Socializing Globalization*", in Boike Rehbein and Klaus W. West (eds.).

Kumar, Anand,(2009), *Paradigm Shift in India : Analyzing the Impact of Liberalization and Globalization*, in Jan Nederveen Peterse and Boike Rehbein (eds). pp 131-141.

Lewis, Oscar., (1958), *Village Life in Northern India*, Illinois, University of Illionois Press.

Liebl M, Roy T, *Handmade in India : Preliminary Analysis of Crafts Producers and Crafts Production*, World Bank, Published in Economic and Political Weekly, 2003.

Liebl, Maureen and Roy, Tirthankar, (2003), *Handmade in India: A Preliminary Analysis of Crafts and Craft Production*, Economic and Political Weekly, Vol. 38, No. 51/52 (Dec 27,2003-Jan. 2, 2004), pp. 5366-5376.

Lok Sabha Un-starred Question No. 1714, Answered on 05.03.2015 on *Handloom Weavers Comprehensive Welfare Schemes* by Ministry of Textiles, Government of India.

Madhok, Bindu, and Selva J. Raj, *"Globalization, Higher Education, And Women In Urban India: A Development Ethics Approach"*, Journal Of Third World Studies 28.1 (2011): 141-154, Academic Search Premier, Web. 16 Jan., 2015.

Mahabharata, Shantiparva, 14, 39,50, 59, Kumbhakonam ed., Vasishtha, Dharmasutra, (Buhler's trans. In SBE, 1882) p. 8, 53 as per *Caste and Race in India* by G. S. Ghurye.

Mahabharata, Anushasana parva, 4, 6, Kumbhakonam ed.

Mathai, John.,*Village Government in British India*, 1915, p 65.

Mandal S.K., (1998), Kumhar/Kumbhar, In Singh, Kumar Suresh, *People of India: Rajasthan*, Popular Prakashan pp. 565-566, ISBN 978-17154-769-2.

Mandalik V. N., *Vyavahara Mayukha*, ed. 1880, p 432.

Manu, *Laws of Manu*, i , 86 (Buhler's trans. in SBE, 1886).

Marx, Karl, *Communist Manifesto*, in Robert Tucker (ed.) (1979), The Marx –Engels Reader, New York : Norton, pp 269-500.

McMichael, Philip, *Development and Social Change: A Global perspective*, Pine Forge Press, 2000.

Mehta, R.J., (1960), *The Handicrafts and Industrial Arts of India*, Published by Bombay: Taraporevala.

Mendelsohn Oliver, Vicziany Marika, *The Untouchables: Subordination, Poverty and the State in Modern India,* Cambridge: Cambridge University Press; 1998.

Mike Featherstone, (1991), *Global culture : Nationalism, Globalization and Modernity*, Vol.2, Sage Publications.

Milner Murray., Jr., *Status and Sacredness: A General Theory of Status Relations and an Analysis of Indian Culture*, New York: Oxford University Press; 1994.

Miletic, Dejan, *Economic globalization through the lens of social scientists and economists*, Economics and Sociology, Belgrade : Institute of Social Sciences, 2007.

Ministry of Education and Social Welfare, Government of India, *Towards Equality, (Report of the Committee on the Status of Women in India)*, 1974, p. 149.

Ministry of Textiles, Govt. of India, *Working Group report on Handicrafts for 12th Five year plan*, 2011: Crafts Council of India, Craft Economics and Impact Study: Stage-1 & Stage-2, 2011.

Mittelman, James, *Globalization and Its Critics*, in: Stubs, Richard and Geoffrey Underhill, Political Economy and the Changing Global Order, Oxford: Oxford University Press, 2006.

Mondal, Biswanath (2004), *"Proceedings of the National Conference on Investment Casting : NCIC2003"*, Allied Publishers, ISBN 81-7764—659-1.

Nagla B.K., *Indian Sociological Thought*, Rawat Publications, ISBN: 81-316-0227-3.

Omvedt, Gail, (2006), *Dalit Visions: The Anti-Caste Movement and the Construction of an Indian Identity,* New Delhi: Orient Longman.

Padmini Sengupta,1960, *Women Workers of India*, Delhi : Asia Publishing House, p. ix.

Pal, P. K., (1978), *Crafts and Craftsmen in Traditional India*, Kanak Publications, New Delhi.

Palanithurai G., Ramesh R., *Globalization : Issues at the Grassroots*, Concept Publishing company , New Delhi-110059.

Panini, M. N., (1997), *The Political Economy of Caste. In Caste: Its Twentieth Century Avatar*, edited by M. N. Srinivas, New Delhi: Penguin Books.

Patanjali, Vyakaranamahabhashya, II, 4, 10, as per *Caste and Race in India* by G.S.Ghurye.

Patil, P.S., *Phooley* (marati) 1927, pp. 25.

Payam Sudhakaran, *"Forgotten Tale of Hammer and Tongs*", Feb., 2nd *Monday* 2015, The Hans India English daily.

Planning Commission: Eleventh Five Year Plan, *Ensuring Rural and urban livelihoods, 2008*, http://planningcommission.gov.in/plans/planrel/fiveyr/11th/11_v3/11v3_ch5.pdf.

Prasad, P.C., (2003), *"Foreign Trade and Commerce in Ancient India"*, Abhinav Publications, ISBN 81-7017-053-2.

Radhakrishna, S., *Death Knell for Handlooms?,* 11thNovember 2007, The Hindu (Sunday Magazine).

Raheja Gloria Goodwin, *India: Caste, Kingship, and Dominance Reconsidered,* Annual Review of Anthropology. 1988;17:497–522.

Ramayana (Nirnayasagar ed.), *Uttarakhanda*, vii, 4, 76.

Ranjan, Aditi and Ranjan, M. P. (Eds), (2007), *Handmade in India: Crafts of India*, co- published by COHANDS and Mapin Publishers Pvt. Ltd., National Institute of Design, Ahmedabad.

Robertson, Roland, *Globalization, Social Theory and Global Culture*, London: Sage, 1992.

Rodrik, Dani (1997), *Has Globalization Gone Too Far?*, Washington: Institute for International Economics.

Rothkopf, D., *In praise of Cultural Imperialism?*, Foreign policy 107, 38-53, 1997.

Roy, M. N., *The Ideal of Indian Womanhood*, Fragments of Prisoner's Diary, Calcutta Renaissance, Publishers Pvt., Ltd., 1957, Vol.1.p 168-71.

Sai Deepak, J., *Protection of Traditional Handicrafts under Indian Intellectual Property Rights*, Journal of Intellectual Property Rights, Vol. 13, May 2008, pp 197- 207.

Saraf, D.N., (1982), *"Indian Craft*", Vikas Publishing House.

Saraf, D.N., Sampark, *In the journey of craft development 1941-1991,* Publication Division, New Delhi, 1991, *p.52.*

Saraswati Baaidyanath (1979), *Pottery-Making Cultures And Indian Civilization*, Abhinav Publications pp 46-47 ISBN 978-81-7017-091-4.

Scrase, T.J. (2003), *Precarious Production : Globalization and Artisan Labour in the Third World*, Third World Quarterly 24(3), p.449-461.

Sennett, Richard, (2008), *The Craftsman*, Yale University Press.

Sahoo, Sarbeswar, *"Globalization And Politics of the Poor in India"*, Journal of Asian & African Studies (Sage Publications, Ltd.) 49.1 (2014): 3-15. Historical Abstracts.Web. 16 Jan., 2015.

Sharma,K.L., *Social Stratification in India: Issues and themes*, Sage Publications, New Delhi 1997, p. 59.

Shrivastava, A., Athavale, M.C., and Gupta, S.K., (1995), *Impact of Non-farm Employment on Income Generation in Similar farms: A case study in Two districts of M.P.*, Indian Journal of Agricultural Economics, 50(3), pp. 448-449.

Srinivas, M. N., (1959), *The Dominant Caste in Rampura*, American Anthropologist, NS, Vol. 61, No.1, pp. 1-16.

Srinivasan, Sharda and Srinivasa Rangnathan, (2004*), India's Legendry Wootz Steel,* Bangalore: Tata Steel, p. 146.

Srinivasan, S.,& Ranganathan, S.*, "Wootz Steel: An Advanced material of the Ancient World,* Indian Institute of Sciences, Bangalore.

Srinivasan, S., (1994), *"Wootz crucible steel: a nearly discovered production site in South India,*Institute of Archaeology, University College London, 5 : 45-61.

Srinivasan, S.,& Griffiths, D., *"South Indian wootz: evidence for high-carbon steel from crucibles from a nearly identified site and preliminary comparisons with related finds"*, Material issues in Art and Archaeology-V, Materials Research Society Symposium Proceedings Series, Vol. 462.

Srivastava, Ravi (2008), *Education, skill and the Emerging Labour Market in India,*The Indian Journal of Labour Economics, 51(4), 759-82.

The Bombay Chronicle, 31st March, 1924.

The Stanford Encyclopedia of Philosophy [SEP], (2006), *Globalization*, http://plato.stanford.edu/entries/globalization/.

Steger, Manfred B., (2009), *Globalization: A very Short Introduction*, NY: Oxford. Stiglitz, J., *Globalization and its Discontents*, Penguin, New York, 2002. *A Study on Craft Economics and Impact Study*, Vol. 1, 2011 by Craft Council of India.

Subramanian, K.K., *An overview of the Handicrafts Industry*, In Subramanian K.K. (ed.), The Handicraft Industry in Kerala: Blending heritage with economics, Dannish Books, Delhi, 2006.

"Suppressions of Traffic in Women and Children and Bengal discussion", Stri Dharma 15, No.12 Oct., 1932, p. 622.

Sutta-Nipata (Fausboll's – translation), pp. 46-51.

Thorat, Sukhdeo, Newman Katherine., editors, *Blocked by Caste: Economic Discrimination in Modern India,* New Delhi: Oxford University Press; 2009.

Upadhyay, M.N., *Handicrafts of India*, Swarajya Printing Works, Secunderabad, 1976.

UNDP: Human Development Report 2011 Sustainability and Equity: A Better Future for All, New York: UNDP; 2011.

UNDP: *Human Development Report 2010 The Real Wealth of Nations. Pathways to Human Development,* New York: UNDP; 2010.

UNESCO, http://portal.unesco.org.

Unni, J., (1998), *Non-Agricultural employment and poverty in rural India – A Review evidence*, Economic and Political Weekly, 33(13), pp. A36-A44.

Varghese K., George (2003), *"Globalization Traumas and new Social imaginary : Visvakarma Community of Kerala"*, Economic and Political Weekly, 38(45).

Vasishtha, Dharmasutra, (Buhler's trans. In SBE, 1882) pp. 5, 7, 8, 9, 25, 16-18, 56, 96, 230, as per *Caste and Race in India* by G. S. Ghurye.

Vasishtha, Dharmasutra, p11; Gautama, pp 224-30; Apastamba, pp. 122-3.

Vedic Index ii p 257, by A Mecdonell and A B Keith, 2 Vols, 1912, as per *Caste and Race in India* by G.S. Ghurye.

Vyakarnamahabhashya I, 2, 72, as per *Caste and Race in India* by G.S. Ghurye.

Wallerstein, Immanuel, *Utopistics: Or, Historical Choices of the Twenty-First Century*, New York: The New York Press, 1998.

Wallerstein, Immanuel, *Globalization or the Age of the Trajectory of the World System*, On line papers, 1999.

Waters, Malcolm, *Globalization*, London and New York: Routledge, 1995.

Weber, Max., *In: The Religion of India: The Sociology of Hinduism and Buddhism*, Gerth H.M., Gelncoe Don, translators. Ill: Free press; 1958. www.blonnet.com. Yajnavalkya, Yajnavalkya smruti, with Mitakshara, ed., by S. S. Setlur, 1912, p. 1165.

Yogendra Singh, *Social Stratification and Change in India*, Manohar, New Delhi 1977, p. 6.

Yousuf Dhamee, (1996), *Adam Smith and Division of Labour*, The Victorian Web, www.victorianweb.org.

Index

A

Abul Fazal, 51
Acquired immuno- deficiency syndrome, 106
Addu Gumme, 131
Adilabad, 53
Aggregation and intermediary trade, 29
Agricultural implements, 140
Agricultural labour, 127
Agricultural Labourer, 147
Agro and Rural Industries, 33
Ain-i-Akbari, 51
Ainapoor, 113
All India Handicrafts Board, 33
All Indian Debt and Investment Survey, 31
Aluminum vessels, 124
Amdapoor, 113
Amrapali a famous Courtesan, 43
Amritsar, 41
Andhra Pradesh, 41
Andhra Pradesh State, 18
Annual income pattern of blacksmiths, 144
Annual income pattern of Potters, 126
Annual income pattern of Weavers, 135
Anthropological accounts of India, 17
Antony Giddens, 89
Apparel Export Parks, 39
Aravallis, 41
Archaeo-Metallurgical, 53
Artisan Caste occupations, 111
Artisan castes, 25
Artisan community, 111
Artisanal Caste occupations, 116
Artisanal Caste production, 111
Arujun Appadurai, 89
Arya Samaj, 81
Asia and Europe, 50
Assistant Director of Handlooms, 45
Atharva Veda, 48
Automobile workshop, 140

B

Baba Sahab Ambedkar Hastshilp Vikas Yojna, 37
Bachhannapet mandal, 147
Backward classes, 112
Badanakall, 113
Ball Mill, Power, 121
Ball-Bearing Sara, 147
Bamboo and cane works, 18
Bangalore tile, 136
Barter system, 149
Basketry, 18
Beating the clay, 123
Bed sheets, 138
Benefits of Earthen cook-ware, 124
Berkeley University, 53
Bidri ware, 38
Blacksmith, 116

Blacksmith communities, 53
Blue pottery of Delhi, 41
Bonala festival, 126
Boycott foreign goods, 28
Brazil, 92
Breakdown of traditional structures, 29
Brhama Samaj, 81
British East India Company, 52
British Raj, 82
British rule, 44
Broad cone rollers, 132
Bronze Age, 50
Bronze vessels, 151
Bronze weapons, 50
Buck Machine, 121
Buddhist Literature, 74, 76
Bullock carts and tools, 140

C

Capital Account, 99
Carpet and floor-coverings, 18
Caste as a system of Exclusion and Exploitation, 68
Caste as Social Construction, 69
Caste as status hierarchy, 68
Caste in Transformation, 69
Caste System, 66
Caste System in India–Praxis, 68
Caste System in Modern Period, 81
Cement Concrete, 127, 136, 145
Cement Concrete" roofs, 136
Centre for Policy Research, Harvard University, 19
Chevella, 113
Chhattisgarh, 111
China, 43
Chinna Cheekodu, 113
Chitikapose Aassu, 131
Chota Nagpur, 41
Classical Anthropological perspective, 66
Cleaning agents, 130
Cloth merchant shops, 135
Cluster approach for specific arts and crafts, 38
Co-operative planning committee, 44
Co-operative society, 45, 137
Coalition government, 106
Collective Mark, 101
Colours for dyeing, 130
Common facility centers, 38
Contemporary Arts and Crafts, 35
Cookery utensils, 153
Copy Rights, 101
Corporate textiles mills, 152
Cosmetic sense, 100
Council for Advancement of People's Action and Rur, 34
Craft Council of India, 21, 23
Craft Economics and Impact Study, 114
Craft Industry, 35
Crafts and Craftsmen in Traditional India, 18
Cultural Economy, 92, 127
Cultural heritage of India, 27
Cultural imperialism, 99
Cultural Phenomena, 70
Cultural Significance, 123
Cup like container, 41
Current Account, 99

D

Damascus Steel, 51
Dastkar Hatt Samiti and Sasha, 36
Deccan plateau, 111
Deemed exporters, 48
Deep frying pans, 153
Defense Industries, 102
Delhi, 41
Department of Jute, 139
Design & Technology up-gradation scheme, 37

Designing sketch of the fabric, 130
Development Commissioner for Handlooms, 36
Development Commissioner Handicrafts, 20, 22, 26
Development Commissioners, 33
Development Commissioners' for Handicrafts, 33
Devendranath Tagore, 81
Devine Draftsman, 49
Dhantheypalugu, 144
Dharma Shastras, 71
Dharma Sutra, 77
Dharmasagar mandal, 146
Division of labour, 64
Diwali toys, 41
Diyas for Deepavali, 42
Dokra metal work, 38
Domestic Economic developments, 104
Domestic markets, 111
Dominance of middlemen, 31
Dosa pans, 153
Drying the utensils in shadow, 123
Dubbaka Mandal, 149
Dwapar Yuga, 49

E

Earthen cookware, 146
Earthen pots, 151
Earthen products, 151
Earthen utensils, 151
East Asia, 92
East India Company, 44
Eco-friendly nature, 118
Egypt, 43
Electric Power cut problems, 134
Electric Power problems, 137
Embroidery, 18
Environment Friendly, 124
Epics testifying contemporary practices, 74
Export of Goods, 98
Extinction of joint family system, 137

F

Fine segregation of the clay, 123
Folk paintings, 18
Foreign Direct Investment, 99, 102
Foreign Universities, 105
Foundations of Indian Economics, 71
Fragmented value chain, 31
Frame looms, 132
France, 43
Fully self-employed artisans, 28

G

Gadwal saris, 38
Gambirpur, 113
Gas Chula, 121
Geographical Indication, 101
Germany, 43
Glazed pottery, 40
Glazed pottery, 40, 41
Glazed pottery of Persian models, 40
Global food chain, 104
Globalization theories, 90
Glory of Indian Handicrafts, 18
Godavari River, 53
Gold brocades, 44
Governor General Bentinck, 44
Grassroots Business Fund, 35
Green Economy, 92
Gross Domestic Product, 19, 92
Gujarat, 21
Gujarat and Maharastra, 40

H

H.H. Risley, 82
Hand-painted fabrics, 18
Handicraft artisans, 34
Handicraft sector, 23
Handicrafts and Industrial Arts of India, 17

Handicrafts Artisan comprehensive Welfare Scheme, 37
Handicrafts Board, 33
Handicrafts in India, 17
Handloom markets, 47
Handloom Officers, 45
Handloom product, 137
Handloom Weavers, 36, 44
Harappa and Mohenjo, 43
Harappa and Mohenjo-Daro, 43
Harappan and Mohenjodaro cultures, 40
Health hazards, 118
Health Insurance Scheme, 36, 37
Health Issues of weavers, 139
Hindu traditional rituals, 42
Hindwani Steel, 51
Historical Perspective, 71
Homo Hierarchicus, 64
Hon Kong, 43
House wife, 150
Human Development Index, 106
Human Development Report, 93
Human immunodeficiency virus, 106
Human Resources Development Scheme, 37
Hyderabad, 51

I

Identification and documentation of arts and craft, 38
IMF and World Bank, 96
Import of Services, 98
Import of Technology, 98
Independent weavers, 45
Indian Artifact Sector, 27
Indian civilization, 109
Indian handicrafts, 22
Indian Institute of Foreign Trade, 21
Indian pottery, 43
Indian pottery Industry, 43
Indian Scenario, 101
Indian Steel, 51
Indian textiles, 43
Indian Universities, 105
Indological Perspective, 70
Indus Valley Civilization, 40, 50
Industrial cooperative societies, 138
Industrial Intermediates, 98
Industrial Revolution, 24, 27
Industrial Weaver's Co-operative Societies, 45
Industrial zones, 143
Industries Development Bank of India, 31
Intellectual Property Rights, 100
International Monetary Fund, 19, 96
International Trade Commission, 101
Iron Pillar, 51
Iron tools and implements, 140
Iron victory pillar of Delhi, 153
Irravat Karve, 67
Italy, 43

J

Jaipur, 41
Janasree Bima Yojana, 34
Jangon town, 148
Japan, 43
Jewelry, 18
Jigger Machine, 121

K

K.K. Subramanian, 32
Kagzi pottery, 42
Kala Raksha and SEWA Ahmedabad, 35
Kali Yuga, 49
Kamaladevi Chattopadhyaya, 23
Kamareddi guda, 113
Kanyakumari, 121
Karigars, 41
Karimnagar, 53, 126

Kerala, 121
Khadi and Village Industries Commission, 21, 34, 121
Khurja, 41
Khurja units, 43
Komaravelly, 113
Kommuravelli village, 122
Konne, 113
Kora chuttadam, 131
Kosgi, 113
Kummargudem, 122

L

Lack of Aggregation, 31
Lavish Multiplex movie halls, 104
Leather works, 18
Liberalization, Privatization and Globalization, 101
LIC of India, 34
Light Scanning, 138
Lingampally villages, 113
Local demand for products, 111
London, 51
Loom Moggam, 131
Lord of all arts, 49
Louis Dumont, 64

M

Maddikunta, 113
Madras School of Economics, 21
Mahabharata, 43
Maharashtra, 111
Mahatma Gandhi Bunkar Bima Yojana, 36, 37
Mahatma Gandhi National Rural Employment Guarantee, 112
Mahatma Jyoti Rao Phule of Poona, 81
Major foreign exchange earner, 129
Makara sankranthi, 41
Mallikudurla village, 113, 122, 146
Marketing assistance and Marketing events, 38
Marketing Support & Services Scheme, 37
Master Craftsmen, 34
Master Weaver, 139
Master Weavers, 46
Master weavers, 137
Master weavers of power looms, 137
Mats, 18
Max Muller, 82
Medak District, 149
Metal and design, 131
Mexico, 43
Middle East, 51
Milton Singer, 61
Ministry of Labour & Employment, 36
Ministry of Rural Development, 33
Ministry of Textiles, 32, 33, 139
Ministry of Tribal Development, 33
Ministry of Women and Child Development, 33
Ministry of Women and Children, 32
Modern Period, 71
Modernization of agriculture, 139
Mohammad al-Idrisi, 51
Mud tile, 136
Mud tile production, 146
Mud tiles, 146
Mughal dynasties, 27
Mughal emperor Akbar, 51
Multi Party, 106
Multinational Corporations, 90, 94
Muslim rulers, 40
Muslims in Northern India, 48
Mustabad Mandal, 122

N

Nanotechnology, 52
Narrow cones, 132
National Accounting Statistics, 114
National Accounting Statistics and Databases, 114, 116

National Bank for Agriculture and Rural Development, 34
National Council of Applied Economic Research, 115, 116
National Cultural Heritage, 101
National Industrial classification categories, 21
National Institute for Advanced Studies, 51
National Sample Survey, 19
National Sample Survey Organization, 115, 116
Native Engineers, 152
Nehru's Industrial modernization programs, 23
Nepal looms, 132
Nepal looms semi-automated, 132
Nets and baskets, 78
New Economic Policy, 102
Nirmal Paintings, 38
Nizamabad, 51, 53
Non-government organizations, 23
North East and Kashmir, 21
Northern Pakistan and Nepal, 48
Northern Telangana, 53, 119
Nuclear type of family, 131

O

Origin of Caste System, 71
Orissa, 41

P

Paper thin pottery, 40
Papier Machse pottery, 42
Part-time artisans, 28
Patents, 101
Peddagundavelli Village, 149
Pembarthy Brass ware, 38
Pepsi and Thums Up bottles, 147
Pit loom, 132
Planning Commission, 20
Plastic bottles, 147
Portuguese and British, 43
Post Vedic Period, 71
Potter Caste profession, 126
Pottery, 18, 116
Pottery in Indian villages, 41, 42
Pottery products, 43
Pottery utensils, 124
Power loom weavers, 39, 134
Pranava Veda, 48
Prarthana Samaj, 81
Pre-loom activities, 139, 148
Pre-loom processes, 132
Primary Weaver's Cooperative Societies, 45
Private Sector, 32
Problems of Indian Artifact Sector, 30
Processing raw yarn, 130
Procuring and processing raw materials, 28

Q

Quantum mechanics, 52

R

Radhakamal Mukherjee, 71
Raja Rajeshwari Temple, 122
Raja Rammohan Roy, 81
Rajasthan, 42
Rajiv Gandhi Shilpi Swasthya Bima Yojana, 34
Ramayana, 43
Rani Chennamma, 52
Rani of Jhansi, 52
Rashtriya Swasthya Bima Yojana, 36
Raw material, 118
Raw silk, 130
Raw silk yarn, 148
Raw yarn, 137
Rekula Kunta Mallana Temple, 122
Religion of India, 61
Research & Development Scheme, 37

Rig-Vedas, 48
Rojagar Youjana, 127
Role of Women, 142
Rome, 43
Royal Commission on Agriculture, 44
Rural artisan, 23
Rural artisanal sector, 152
Rural India, 27
Rural Telangana region, 137
Rural weavers, 137
Rural workforce, 19
Rural youth, 32
Russia, 92

S

Sacred laws of Aryans, 73
Sama Veda, 48
Satyashodhak Samaj, 81
School teacher, 150
Self Help Groups, 112
Sepoy mutiny, 52
Service Castes, 25
Sexual harassments, 103
Sexual symbols, 100
Shaivet Temples, 126
Sickels, 144
Silk and Cotton fabrics, 44
Silk and fabric production, 151
Silk saris, 137, 148
Sir Charles Eliot, 77
Skill up gradation and quality improvement, 38
Skilled master artisans, 28
Small Industries Development Bank, 31
Small Industries Development Bank of India, 34
Small-scale industries, 104
Soaking the clay, 123
Social Anthropologist Perspective, 70
Social Stratification, 66
Sociology for India, 61
Son of Brahma, 49
Sone ki Lanka, 49
South India, 43
Southern Telangana, 119
Special Economic Zone, 143
Structural – Functional Perspective, 69
Structural Phenomena, 70
Stry of Textiles to Ministry, 32
Substantializaton of Castes, 64
Sun Set Industry, 33
Supplies the yarn, 48
Swadeshi movement, 23
Swami Dayanand, 81
Swami Vivekananda, 81

T

Tamil Nadu, 21, 41
Tata Iron and Steel, 52
Technological aspects, 133, 142
Technology upgrading and design support centers, 38
Teflon non-stick cookware, 153
Telangana region, 53, 121, 132, 133, 135, 142
Telangana State, 39
Telangana State Handicrafts and Artisans Revival w, 39
Terlumaddi, 113
Terlumadi village, 122
Terracotta, 18
Terracotta figures, 41
Textile Industry, 129
Textile traders, 137
Textiles, 18
Thangallapalli Sudarshana Chary, 149
Thatched roof, 136
Thatched roof" houses, 136, 145
Thelma Lowe, 53
Tipu Sultan, 52, 153
Toddy pots, 146
Tractors and machineries, 140

Trade Marks, 101
Trade Secrets, 101
Traders and Exporters, 34
Traditional artisanal production, 129
Traditional blacksmith, 140
Traditional blacksmiths, 140
Traditional caste occupation, 149
Traditional Cultural Expressions, 101
Traditional handloom weavers, 152
Traditional Indian women, 104
Traditional looms, 139
Traditional occupation, 151
Traditional pottery artisans, 128
Traditional production method, 136
Trans-National corporations, 95
Treta Yuga, 49

U

Ultra High Carbon Steel, 52
UN agencies and Action Aid, 19
UN organized production, 30
Understanding of Globalization, 95
UNESCO frame works, 26
Unglazed pottery, 40
Unhygienic working conditions, 103
United Nations, 24, 113
United Nations Development Programme, 93
University of Minnesota, 19
Utility Models, 101
Uttar Pradesh, 41, 43

V

Vedic Period, 71
Vemulawada, 122
Vikarabad, 113
Village and Small Scale Industries Committee, 45
Viswakarma caste, 53
Vocational training schools, 109

W

Wage worker artisans, 28
Warangal, 53, 146
Warangal carpets, 38
Warangal district, 147
Warp and Weft, 130
Water rings, 144
Water storage, 146
Watershed Development, 112
Weaver, 116
Weavers' Co-operatives, 44
Weavers of Telangana, 137
Western ideologies, 100
Western Sciences, 100
Women and Children, 32
Women Artisans, 111
Women of Bihar, 41
Wootz Steel, 50, 51, 52, 153
Working Group report on Handicrafts, 33
World Bank, 96
World Intellectual Property Organization, 101
World Trade Organization, 96
Woven textiles, 18

Y

YajurVeda, 48
Yogender Singh, 63

Z

Zari, Silver, 44